"Lee Hord brings together concepts of personal performance and life skills in a fun and energizing read. His book, Eating Elephants, Living a Life of Impact Performance! is filled with ways to enhance personal performance and become focused on the life categories of health, relationships, careers, and finance. One of the benefits of using this book is the emphasis on individual responsibility for personal satisfaction. It does indeed create a model to structure your belief system, which impacts life's outcomes."

Dr. B. James Dawson, President
Lincoln Memorial University

"If you want to improve your life one bite at a time, I would highly recommend Eating Elephants, Living a life of Impact Performance! I wish I had an opportunity to read this book in my early adult life. Eating Elephants guides you to understand that balance in health, relationships, career, and finances allows for personal growth and Impact Performance! Learning how to help others to succeed is the greatest benefit of reading this book. Start today – improve your life and others NOW."

Dr. Teresa Resch, Senior VP of Academic Excellence
Medtech

Praise from Elephant Eaters...

"...inspiring, a great motivator...excellent at building confidence...I now have a guide to help me focus on what is important...it is a road map through the highways of life, without a map people tend to get lost...I have been lost, now I know which direction to drive...it shows people how to succeed in life."

— Lloyd L.

"I had already set goals for myself...now I am more organized and able to reach them."

— Kelsey F.

"It helped me get out of my shell...thanks for believing in me and pushing me to achieve more."

— Cassie G.

"I consider Lee a trusted advisor, visionary, and devourer of elephants."

— Joshua P.

Eating Elephants

Living a life
of
Impact Performance!

Lee Alan Hord, Sr.

INFINITY
PUBLISHING

Copyright © 2011 by Lee Alan Hord, Sr.

ISBN 0-7414-6902-2 Paperback
ISBN 0-7414-6903-0 eBook
Library of Congress Control Number: 2011939550

Printed in the United States of America

Published December 2011

INFINITY PUBLISHING
1094 New DeHaven Street, Suite 100
West Conshohocken, PA 19428-2713
Toll-free (877) BUY BOOK
Local Phone (610) 941-9999
Fax (610) 941-9959
Info@buybooksontheweb.com
www.buybooksontheweb.com

Eating Elephants is dedicated to Alan and Holly.

Additionally this work is dedicated to future
Elephant Eaters and Elephant Hunters;
may you live a life
of
Impact Performance!

Acknowledgements

I would like to thank the following for their inspiration and ongoing motivational support; they helped make *Eating Elephants...Living a Life of Impact Performance!* a reality.

I am forever grateful to Ramon Presson who helped me realize that anything is possible. You are a true elephant hunter, my friend. A special thanks to James H. Brown whose demonstration of always doing the right thing has been a guiding light through the years. To Tag Graham, thank you for being in my boat, for your enduring friendship and branding support (www.pgdg.com) of Impact Performance!

I appreciate my supportive family and their undying love. You are always in my heart and thoughts. Finally yet importantly, I want to thank my students who have given me the opportunity to repay the debt of instruction and guidance I have received along life's journey.

Contents

Appendix

impact!
PERFORMANCE
Define ▸ Analyze ▸ Energize

www.ip-getmoving.com

Foreword by Ramon L. Presson

Therapist & Author of *When Will My Life Not Suck? Authentic Hope for the Disillusioned*

Eating elephants is probably not your idea of fine dining. The flavor is suspect and the texture is a bit tough. Not to mention the portions are so large. On the other hand, while you will look much more sophisticated savoring tiny bites of a soufflé, you will be hungry again in an hour. Eating an elephant is very filling...and fulfilling, because it is such an accomplishment.

Lee Hord has written an outstanding chef and diner's guide to cooking and eating the elephants that are taking up so much space in your professional and personal life that you need to either evict them or start charging them rent.

Steven Pressfield in his book *The War of Art* is adamant that we will always be waging war against Resistance - a force that appears in many forms seeking to delay, block, or even push back against your advancement to accomplish anything of significance. For you, in your personal and professional growth and development, the resistance will most often come from inside you. Mark this down: there is never significant growth, no breakthroughs and no profound success apart from overcoming the troops of resistance that will show up on your frontlines the moment you wake and your feet touch the floor.

The elephant blocking your path will not move by invoking some mystical secret law from an over-hyped book. Nor will he evaporate by touching him with the magic wand from a motivational speaker. You have to eat the elephant out of its very existence in the road. In addition, Joshua would tell you that task is both an outside job and an inside job. Lee Hord will tell you in this book that you have external work to do and you have internal work to do. What I appreciate is that Lee guides you through the process.

One of the things that makes Lee an excellent and credible tour guide is that he himself has implemented the very process he describes. He was the rocket's test pilot and it soared. How do I know that? Because I remember years ago when Lee first approached me with his idea for this book, the desire to share with others what he had learned and experienced. I can tell you from firsthand experience as an author of several books myself that the writing and publishing of any book is walking up to an elephant with a fork and spoon. Writing a book is having the attitude of David with a slingshot confronting your Goliath. Lee worked the plan in his life BEFORE he ever set out to write this book, what I will call the equivalent of getting his master's degree in credibility. Then he actually did what many aspire to do but never start OR start but never finish; he wrote and published his book. In my mind, this earned Lee Hord his doctorate in credibility.

Reading this book will not be enough. There is no blessing from having mere knowledge. In fact, often, increased knowledge creates more stress as you become aware of the gap between your knowledge and your action. Nothing short of thoughtful and intentional implementation of the principles in this book will change anything. You cannot apply and implement it all. You will not activate everything all at once. Nevertheless, you have to start. Moreover, you have to keep moving. I have a math equation that goes like this: Passivity + Procrastination = Zero. What will you get in your professional and personal life if you are passive instead of proactive, if you procrastinate instead of pursue? Nothing. You will get absolutely nothing.

Sometimes my grandmother would say at the end of dinner, "Keep your fork." I knew that meant dessert was coming! I want to say to you, "Read this book. Think through the implications and applications according to your needs. Then do it; eat the elephant. And when you're done...keep your fork because you're going to love what's for dessert!"

Ramon Presson

"The ultimate measure of a man is not where he stands in moments of comfort and convenience, but where he stands at times of challenge and controversy."

Martin Luther King, Jr.

"All truths are easy to understand once they are discovered; the point is to discover them."

Galileo

"The unexamined life is not worth living."

Socrates

Prologue, Author's Note

"You can't do that!" "It can't be done." "It's impossible!"

That is precisely what I was told when setting out to write this book. I was told it is impossible to develop a model that could facilitate personal performance improvement across a broad spectrum of people. This challenge only served to fuel my desire to do just that, to deliver a guide for you to deliver Impact Performance! in your life and in the lives of others.

I have witnessed too much human potential and energy forever wasted. I am compelled, as a performance expert, to help you excel in life. Anyone can improve their personal performance by eliminating that which stands in their way; that is, to eat the elephant. The key point to any performance improvement effort is to measure and demonstrate improvement. Keep in mind "performance is reality." The intention is for you to eat the elephant and demonstrate your personal improvement to yourself and others.

I trust you will savor this dining experience. I look forward to sharing your success story in which to inspire others to eat the elephant as well.

Bon appetite and get moving!

Lee

Key Impact Performance! Definitions

We will begin with key definitions referenced throughout *Eating Elephants, Living a Life of Impact Performance!*

IMPACT – The acronym that constitutes the Impact Mission-Values Statement; part of your strategy to live a life of Impact Performance!

Impact Performance! – Ongoing measurable personal performance improvement resulting from the adoption of the Impact Performance! - Personal Improvement Model (IP!-PIM) and principles herein; the insatiable Elephant Eater's appetite for life.

Elephants – The seemingly, intimidatingly, daunting immovable people, places, things (patterns), and circumstances that block individuals from achieving; elephants are the identifiable obstacles you target and overcome to improve performance and achieve Impact Success.

Elephant Eaters – Individuals who want to eat the elephant; those who desire to live a life of Impact Performance!

Elephant Hunters – Elephant Eaters who have eaten the elephant and who help others improve their personal performance.

The Impact Team – The team of Elephant Hunters committed to improving the lives of others using the Impact Performance! principles.

Life Categories – The four key categories of life that comprise overall personal performance; Life Categories are equally weighted and interconnected; the balance across these categories is a key to overall performance improvement and Impact Success; the Life Categories are:

- Health
- Relationships
- Career
- Finances

Life's Outcomes – The resultant outcome and performance level of each of the respective Life Categories; the outputs of the Self-System.

Impact Goals – The stated goals strived for in each of the Life Categories; same as Life Category Goals.

Impact Objectives – The target date of eating elephants in each of the Life Categories; eating the elephant propels you along the *Impact Performance!* Continuum and demonstrates personal performance improvement.

Impact Performance! – *Personal Improvement Model (IP!-PIM)* – The guiding principles and actionable steps to achieve measurable personal performance improvement and to eat elephants.

Impact Mission-Values Statement – the foundation for personal performance improvement; a strategy for living Impact Performance!

The Impact Action Plan – Your personal action plan to achieve your stated Impact Objectives (i.e. eat the elephant date) and performance milestones.

Impact Performance! Continuum – The visual representation of your overall performance and the Life Category performance levels.

Success – Redefined by Impact Performance! standards; achieved by making progress toward the Impact Goals, a performance focus, and striving for balance across the Life Categories.

Performance Focus – The positive thought patterns, conversations, decisions, behaviors and actions directed toward the Impact Goals; a key determinate of Impact Success.

Self-System – A person's overall performance system that is comprised of inputs, a process, outcomes, and a measurement mechanism in which to take action-control for continuous improvement.

Power Source – That which fuels Self-Leadership; the inputs to the Self-System comprised of Energy, Desire – the will to succeed, Intrinsic Motivation, and Courage.

Self-Leadership – The process of the Self-System that produces outcomes (Life's Outcomes) from the inputs (Power Source); comprised of Thought Patterns, Decision-Making Paradigms, Behaviors, and Actions.

Measurement – Daily journal entries, Accountability Partner feedback, and the Mentoring used to monitor and track improvement over time; affords action-control.

Journaling – Written summary of the actions taken towards reaching the Impact Objectives, Impact Goals and performance milestones along the Impact Performance! Continuum; affords tracking of Impact Performance!

The Impact Performance! Journal – The personal journal of Elephant Eaters who log daily entries; this journal has entry points for each of the Life Categories, the Power Source, Self-Leadership, and overall Impact Performance! tracking.

Accountability Partner – The trusted partner who acts as a mirror to reflect your performance improvement efforts; the one who holds you accountable for eating the elephant and provides on-going support.

Mentors – The persons who provide guidance in the Life Categories; Elephant Eaters may have more than one mentor.

Elephants

There are people, places, things and circumstances standing in your way of achieving personal improvement; i.e. elephants. You eat the elephant, never to return; as such, you achieve breakthroughs in personal performance.

People

There are people in your life that may be holding you back. Identify them, reduce their influence, and include only those who promote positive outcomes in your sphere. Eliminate the persons who influence you in a negative way from your life. At least minimize their ability to influence your thoughts, decisions, behaviors, and actions. As the saying goes, "If you want to be successful, surround yourself with successful people."

Who is influencing your thought? Who invokes negative emotion? Who gives you bad advice or leads you to negative outcomes?

We will discuss who is in your "boat" later. The point is to include only those who influence you in a positive way to promote positive outcomes in your life.

Places

There are environments in which you live that may create negative outcomes. As such, eliminate negative spatial environments and seek environments that promote positive outcomes.

Often, environments can create negative feelings. For example, people who live in northern extremes such as Sweden have a higher tendency for depression which is believed to be due to lack of sunshine (called seasonal affective disorder or SAD, no pun intended here). On the other hand, artists tend to find environments that release their talent (e.g. Hemingway spent winters in Key West and summers in Wyoming during much of the 1930's).

Think of the places where you exist. Do these environments promote your ability to excel and achieve?

"Places" refers to the actual spatial setting where you exist. These locations include your home, place of work, place of worship, where you exercise, where you relax, etc. Certain types of scenery can help put your life in perspective (e.g. hiking).

Where you physically place yourself influences your Life's Outcomes. Where are you? Are your "places" facilitating positive outcomes?

Things (patterns)

There are tangible patterns in your life that may be holding you back or limiting your ability to excel. As such, change those patterns in a positive way to promote positive outcomes. It is likely you have vices in your life that hold you hostage. What are the patterns that create negative outcomes in your life? What are the negative patterns of behavior that have led to your current level of performance?

The obvious negative pattern examples are smoking and eating disorders. You have patterns of managing your health, relationships, career and finances that have led to your current overall performance level. Your patterns contribute to predictable performance outcomes. You must change your negative patterns to positive patterns, which increases the probability of positive outcomes.

Circumstances

There are circumstances or situations that may limit your sight and hold you back. Your current situation is a result of every thought, decision, conversation, behavior and action you have taken in your life. Yes, there are circumstances that are out of your control. Do not waste time or worry about circumstances that are out of your control when improving personal performance. Focus on what you can control and seek guidance as necessary to know the difference between what is controllable and that which is not.

Change your circumstances in a positive way to promote positive outcomes.

Which situations cause you the most negative outcomes? Do you find yourself in certain social situations due to a need for social acceptance only to find, in the end, it was a negative experience?

We have all heard someone was lucky in terms of being in the "right place at the right time." You can increase the probability of positive outcomes by creating positive circumstances. As in the game of chess, one positions the pieces strategically for both offensive and defensive purposes to increase the probability of victory. Position yourself to win by creating positive circumstances.

Perhaps you over invested in a home or accepted a toxic relationship and feel trapped? Perhaps you made a poor career choice? Do you suffer wellness problems due to poor behavioral choices? In whatever circumstance you presently find yourself, you have the power to change that circumstance to yield and demonstrate positive improvement.

Grab your fork. Now is the time to identify, confront, and eat the elephant!

1

The Menu

An Introduction to Impact Performance!

"Performance is your reality. Forget everything else."

Harold S. Geneen

Impact Performance! is for everyone. No matter your present station in life or present circumstance, you can achieve greater performance outcomes and live a life of Impact Performance! Your nationality, race, religion, sexual orientation, political views, your looks, net worth, and your opinions do not matter. Demonstrated measurable performance is your reality.

Impact Performance! is your ability to develop and live a process that yields continuous personal performance improvement. Here you will achieve the ability to measure your Impact Performance! and help others to achieve as well. You are on a new pathway of living. To live a successful life that is full of Impact means that you improve performance in each of the Life Categories, live with a performance focus and strive for balance across Life's Categories. Elephant Eaters measure their performance and take action-control to improve performance in each of Life's Categories.

A performance focus with measurable and demonstrable improvement results across the Life Categories is a clear path to greater personal achievement in any endeavor you undertake. The improvement model presented in *Eating Elephants, Living a life of Impact Performance!* is proven in helping you reach your Impact Goals with improved Life Outcomes. Importantly, we are inviting you to become part of something greater than yourself; that is, to help others achieve Impact Performance! as well.

Every person can improve their Life's Outcomes - i.e. their performance in each of the Life Categories. There are countless self-help books and most people know fundamentally that their negative thoughts, decisions, behaviors and actions produce poor results. So why do most people continue to live a sub-optimal life? Most people are not well equipped, not well guided and not committed enough to sustain positive change. They are simply unable to eat the elephant.

The good news is that all of us can develop a process for continual personal performance improvement. In *Eating Elephants*, we address the reasons for sub-optimal personal performance:

1. Lack of elephant identification and / or denial of that which stands in the path of improvement
2. Lack of a performance focus on the Power Source, Self-Leadership and the Life Categories (i.e. the Self-System)
3. Imbalance across the Life Categories
4. Lack of measurement and tracking
5. Minimal alignment of actions to goals

6. Minimal accountability (denial of consequences)
7. Lack of on-going motivation and support

What are elephants? Why eat the elephant?

Elephants hold you back from accomplishing and achieving. They stand intimidatingly in your way. Elephants are the number one reason for sub-optimal performance. Elephants limit us in every way possible and ultimately define us. There are times when elephants can defeat us, if we let them. Assuredly, we shall eat these elephants - hence, never to appear again. There is nothing that you cannot accomplish, once you conquer that which constrains you and limits your potential.

Elephants appear daunting; we become paralyzed to the point we cannot see beyond them. Our vision becomes limited and defined by that which stands in our way. We yield, acquiesce, become stymied and stagnant; we live constrained and programmed. Most of us do not know how to overcome simply because we were never taught a process for continual personal improvement. Unfortunately, we settle for subpar performance.

If you were to conquer your greatest fear, would you not become more capable of overcoming any adversity you face or achieving anything you desire? Open your mind and your heart to the possibilities.

There is no problem or challenge so big or intimidating that you cannot solve it and overcome it once you break it down into its component parts and digest those smaller pieces.

In *Eating Elephants,* you will learn how to apply proven principles to achieve personal performance improvement with demonstrable results by breaking down your performance across the Life Categories into respective sub-categories. The Impact Team is here to help you eat the elephant, institute a process for continuous improvement, and achieve greater Life Outcomes. If you are saying to yourself, "Oh no, not another self-help book," soon you'll be proclaiming, "Wow, this is not another self-help book." You know you have the ability to produce greater Life Outcomes. You know that negative thought patterns and negative behaviors yield negative outcomes. Here we are going to adopt a performance focus and hold ourselves accountable with no more excuses.

Why focus on my performance? Why try to improve? What is in it for me?

These are legitimate questions. To be clear, there is no such thing as maintaining the status quo or a free lunch. You are going up or going down, progressing or regressing, never stagnant. Since life is ever changing in every way, you have to adopt a success model to manage change; else, change will manage you. You are either a victim of circumstance or a master of your destiny. It is your choice. We are here to help. Ultimately, you are the one who will earn it.

The three primary reasons to adopt the Impact Performance! - Personal Improvement Model (IP!-PIM):

1. Help yourself to achieve personal performance improvement
2. Satisfy basic human needs
3. Help others to achieve personal performance improvement

"The greatest deed is to help others succeed." To help others, we must first learn to help ourselves. Once our house is in order, we can help others to learn to help themselves. When you have given someone the ability to gain dignity and improve their life, there is no greater level of satisfaction and recognition of your purpose.

Every person has the capacity to look beyond him or herself and help others. First we need to adopt the IP!-PIM and demonstrate progress. Then we can reach-out to others and share Impact Performance! When you help others succeed, you help yourself in ways that money and riches cannot deliver.

The spirit of living a life of Impact Performance! is that you will more predictably satisfy your basic human needs and help others achieve as well. There are no guarantees, but the more effort you put into living a life of Impact Performance! the more you shall gain.

Further Arguments for Personal Performance Improvement

These alarming statistics provide additional context for the need of personal performance improvement in our lives:

Suicide (www.nih.gov)

- The rate of suicide in the U.S. per 100,000 increased from 10.46 to 11.26 from 1999 to 2007 based on Centers for Disease Control (CDC) data.
- Suicide was the tenth leading cause of death in the U.S. in 2007.
- Suicide is the third leading cause of death among young adults.

Depression

- More than a million people aged over 65 suffer clinical depression. As the population ages, more and more of our elderly will suffer.
- Nearly 10% of the U.S. population suffers from some form of depression.
- Teenagers are at risk for depression. The evidence is in teen suicide rates, which are increasing yearly. Low self-esteem can lead to a negative perspective of life and depression.

Chronic Diseases (Centers for Disease Control)

- Seven out of ten deaths among Americans each year are from chronic diseases. Most chronic illnesses can be avoided with proper behavioral changes and properly managed via clinical intervention models.

Diabetes (www.nih.gov)

- Diabetes affects 25.8 million people of all ages. That is 8.3% of the U.S. population.
- For ages 20 and above, 25.6 million or 11.3% of this population in the U.S. have this disease (18.8 million diagnosed and 7 million undiagnosed).
- In 2005–2008, based on fasting glucose or hemoglobin A1C (blood glucose) levels, 35 percent of U.S. adults ages 20 years or older and 50 percent of adults ages 65 years or older had pre-diabetes. Applying this percentage to the entire U.S. population in 2010 yields an estimated 79 million American adults ages 20 years or older with pre-diabetes.

- Diabetes is the leading cause of kidney failure, non-traumatic lower-limb amputations, and new cases of blindness among adults in the United States.
- Diabetes is a major cause of heart disease and stroke.
- Diabetes is the seventh leading cause of death in the United States.

Heart Disease

- Heart disease is the number one cause of death.
- One fifth of all hospitalizations have a primary or secondary diagnosis of heart failure.

Eating Disorders (www.anad.com)

- Almost 50% of people with eating disorders meet the criteria for depression.
- Only 1 in 10 men and women with eating disorders receive treatment.
- Up to 24 million people of all ages and genders suffer from an eating disorder (anorexia, bulimia and binge eating disorders) in the United States.
- Eating disorders have the highest mortality rate of any mental illness.

Obesity (www.cdc.gov)

- Approximately 17% (or 12.5 million) of children and adolescents aged 9 – 12 years are obese.
- Since 1980, obesity prevalence among children and adolescents has almost tripled.
- About 1/3 of adults are obese.

- Obesity related health conditions include heart disease, stroke, type 2 diabetes, and certain types of cancers (some of the leading causes of death).
- In 2008, health care costs associated with obesity were estimated at $147 billion. The medical costs for those who are obese were $1,429 higher than those of normal weight (i.e. % body fat).

Personality Disorders

- 9.1% of the U.S. population meets the criteria for a personality disorder.

Relationships

- One in three teenagers has experienced violence in a dating relationship (www.acadv.org).
- 40+% of first marriages will end in divorce; 60+% of second marriages will end in divorce; 70+% of third marriages will end in divorce.
- Lack of effective and efficient communication is a primary reason for divorce.

Career

- Over half of employees are dissatisfied with their job.
- In the next six months, 60% of workers will search for another job (salary.com survey).
- The typical worker will have nine different jobs by age 32 (U.S. Bureau of Labor Statistics).

Finances

- Most in the U.S. live paycheck to paycheck.

- Almost 45% have less than $25,000 in savings and investments (aside from equity in primary residences).
- Over 50% always or sometimes worry about their finances.
- Financial stress is a leading cause for divorce.

The statistics given above paint a very sad picture indeed. What is truly sad is that most of the statistics given above are controllable and avoidable.

You are most likely experiencing sub-optimal performance in your health, relationships, career, and / or finances. Is this what you desire or is this the expected outcome from your life's work and experiences?

The great news is that it is possible to improve your Health, Relationships, Career, and Finances Performance levels. You can improve Life's Outcomes and help change the statistics.

We live in a culture of low expectations, where mediocrity is accepted. We are influenced by individualism, materialism and consumerism. It is as if most believe that our actions have no consequences. We must change. An axiom in performance improvement: to change outcomes, we must change the inputs and the system itself that yield those outcomes. It is not always easy to change; it takes effort. If you are willing, there is a way to greater performance and improved outcomes.

We cannot solve all the problems we face as humans. You will not suddenly or magically become a new person by following this guide. The intention is to achieve demonstrable performance results and improved life outcomes on a continuous basis. The level of improvement is up to you. How much effort, energy and focus are you willing to expend? The IP!-PIM and the Impact Performance! principles presented here are intended to give you a process by which you can demonstrate personal performance improvement by:

- Eliminating that which stands in your way of achieving your Impact Goals; that is, to eat the elephant;
- Closing the gaps between your Impact Goals across the Life Categories and current performance levels;
- Improving your Power Source and Self-Leadership;
- Maintaining a performance focus;
- Striving for balance, and
- Measuring performance and proactively taking action-control on an on-going basis.

As such, you, as a force of one, can make a difference in your life and the lives of others within your sphere of influence. Perhaps with growing confidence, you can indeed live a life of Impact Performance! and together, we can change the statistics?

What to do?

Our rally cry is, "eat the elephant" so it can never appear again. It is not enough to try to avoid them or go around them; we have to eliminate them altogether. If you are thinking, "I can't" at this point, then please continue your pursuit of Impact Performance! because you can. We are here to help you succeed.

Recall the old saying, "How do you eat an elephant?" The answer is of course, "One bite at a time", which is appropriate for problem solving. Recall that elephants hold us back from achieving and living up to our potential. To eat the elephant we must break down the elephant into digestible pieces and eat them one bite at a time.

The Impact principles presented here afford a systematic guide to eating your elephants. This is a guide and a reference for on-going improvement. The intention is to put you on-track for measureable personal performance improvement – ultimately to live a life of Impact Performance! To achieve and maintain high levels of performance requires:

- A declaration and vision of the person you want to be
- A definition of where you are today and where you are going
- An action plan to close the performance gap
- A measurement system that reflects progress
- And, an on-going motivation and a support structure.

You are not alone in this endeavor. The Impact Team provides support to Elephant Eaters, like you, via our blog (http://blog.ip-getmoving.com) and our Facebook page (www.facebook.com/impactperformance). The Impact Team provides ongoing performance tips and commentary to support your improvement efforts. Elephant Eaters and Elephant Hunters are encouraged to provide suggestions and commentary on the various topics to support their fellow Elephant Eaters. A solid support structure is a pillar of continuous performance improvement. Life is a jungle at times and we need help to take down the elephants.

Note there are all types of people in every circumstance imaginable. We are all connected and have basic human traits in terms of our needs, desires, potential and response to stimuli. To be clear, each of us has latent potential and untapped capacity to achieve greater outcomes in our life. Every person can improve and do more to help others.

We desire to facilitate and nurture your ability to demonstrate progress with positive outcomes and the ability to help others. Note we will redefine success not by societal standards or in comparison to others' standards but by demonstrating improvement. Every Elephant Eater has the ability to be successful in their own right and to celebrate their progress and achievement of their milestones. The first step on the path of success is a desire to succeed. You are on the path to improvement success if you have the desire.

Some basic personal performance questions:

Are you satisfied with where you are today? Do you know where you are going and how to get there? Do you have a vision for the future? Do you have a mission-values statement?

Are you balanced across the Life Categories?

Are you making progress towards your goals in each Life Category? Do you have an improvement plan for each Life Category?

Do you have a measurement system that affords you and others to see your progress? How do you know when to take action-control?

Are you able to summon the Power to overcome the obstacles that hold you back? Do you have the self-awareness and self-control to take the initiative to change as needed to improve?

Are you healthy in mind, body and spirit?

Do you have the right people in your "boat" to help you to achieve your stated goals? If not, do you have the power to get the right people in your boat and make those who are not "walk the plank"?

Do you have passion for your career? Do you seek more challenge and growth opportunities in your profession?

Do you have a budget and stick to it? Do you have a positive net worth? Do you give to charity?

Do you help others succeed and improve their lives?

If you could not answer definitively with a resounding "yes" to these questions above, then we can and want to help. The value of this book and of the Impact Team is that you will be able to answer all the Impact questions above with confidence. You will experience progress soon with the IP!-PIM guide.

Are you willing to do what it takes to change and to be the person capable of helping others? Do you want to eat the elephant?

Yes! Then, let us eat. Get moving!

2

The Appetizers

Your Life Viewed as a System, Basic Human Needs and the Impact Performance! Continuum

The Self-System

You can think of your life as a system. Systems have inputs and a process that produce outputs. On the next page, is the illustration of The Self-System:

Life Viewed as a System

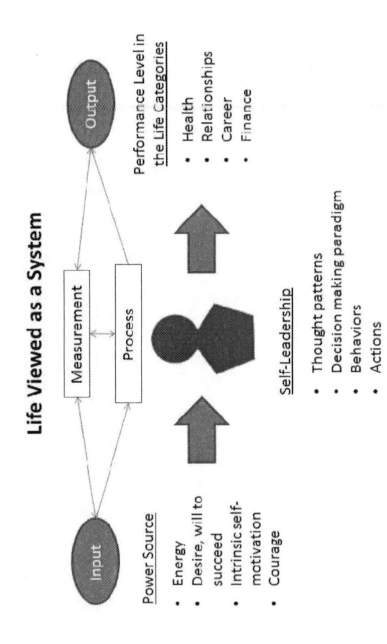

Input

Measurement

Process

Output

Power Source

- Energy
- Desire, will to succeed
- Intrinsic self-motivation
- Courage

Self-Leadership

- Thought patterns
- Decision making paradigm
- Behaviors
- Actions

Performance Level in the Life Categories

- Health
- Relationships
- Career
- Finance

The Power Source combined with Self-Leadership yields predictable performance in the Life Categories. To improve personal performance across the Life Categories, we must improve our Power Source and improve our Self-Leadership. Measurement affords effective positive action-control. Action-control means we are going to take the appropriate action from the measurement feedback to better control the Self-System - i.e. continuous improvement.

The Power Source (input) is your inner fuel; it is your energy, the desire and will to succeed, intrinsic motivation and courage to eat the elephant. Self-Leadership (the process) is comprised of your thought patterns, decision-making paradigm, behaviors and actions taken. The output produced by your process equates to your levels of performance as measured in the Life Categories: Health, Relationships, Career and Finances.

Life Category performance levels are dictated by the combination of the ability to summon the *Power* needed to face adversity and *Self-Leadership* to overcome that adversity.

Note that extrinsic forms of motivation do not yield long-term Impact Performance!; no, it is your inner drive and ability to activate the Power Source, which fuels performance improvement. Extrinsic motivators will not deliver sustainable change to your Self-Leadership. It is your self-awareness and self-control fueled by your Power Source that yields sustainable Self-Leadership change and thus, the ability to improve Life's Outcomes.

You are programmed how to live and react to stimuli; thus outcomes are predictable. You are where you are today due to the culmination of every thought, every spoken word, every decision and every action you have taken in your life. Your Self-System has patterns that have to change to reap the rewards of Impact Performance! You have to effect positive change now to create positive outcomes in the future.

What is usually missing from the Self-System? It is the act of measuring performance in the Life Categories and taking proper action to create desired positive outcomes. Measurement provides the feedback needed to actuate on-going action-control of your Power Source and Self-Leadership. Soon you will institute a conscious and tangible measurement system that will make you more aware of the ramifications of your actions. Are your thoughts, decisions, behaviors, spoken words and actions aligned to achieving your Impact Goals? Do you possess the will and courage to succeed? Are you conscious of the ramifications of your thought patterns, conversations, behaviors, and actions?

You may not be aware, but you can effect positive change to yield desired life outcomes by proper adjustment and management of the Self-System. How do you know what to adjust, how to adjust and by how much? You need a measurement system and a feedback loop in order for you to take action-control of your life. We will focus on your performance measurement system and the actions needed to produce desired outcomes.

By adopting the Impact Performance! - Personal Improvement Model you are expressing leadership over the Self-System. You will focus on the categories of life that truly matter and make a positive difference in each. Elephant Eaters take control and become leaders of their lives. They become conscious of the Self-System and adopt a performance focus to produce desired resultant outcomes.

To change your Life's Outcomes, you must change your negative thought patterns, change your inner and spoken conversations, your decisions and change your actions. In addition, you must improve the ability to engage the Power Source to fuel Self-Leadership properly given any situation. You must identify elephants and devour them. The Impact Team knows it is not easy to change as you are programmed by historical events, low expectations, societal norms, the way you see yourself and your perception of your current circumstances. These are strong forces, but you can overcome anything if you desire to do so. Everyone who desires positive change needs inspiration, on-going motivation, the proper tools, coaching and support. We are here to help.

Our lives are a system; as such, we can improve. Recognize your life as a system in which you can take more control and you are well on your way to improved results.

Elephants exist across every facet of the Self-System. You eliminate these elephants to avail yourself to greater levels of performance. We identify the elephants to eliminate them. As you go forward, keep the Self-System in mind: Power Source, Self-Leadership, Life's Outcomes, and measurement. Be on the lookout for those Elephants; they exist.

Basic Human Needs, Maslow's Hierarchy

"A person starts to live when he can live outside himself."

Albert Einstein

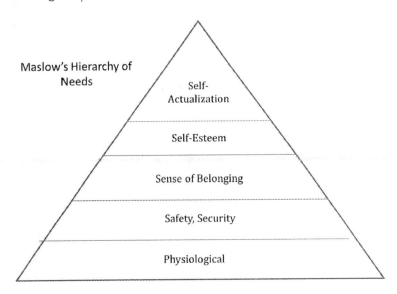

Maslow's Hierarchy of Needs

Self-Actualization

Self-Esteem

Sense of Belonging

Safety, Security

Physiological

Most of us have heard of Maslow's hierarchy of needs. Recall the top of the human needs pyramid. It is self-actualization, which means to experience who we truly are, to find and experience purpose in our lives and to realize our potential.

Along the path of Impact Performance! you will envision a better "self" and live as such. We will spend time and focus on the Power Source. That is, your ability to tap into your source of Power on command will create a greater sense of self. When you push yourself, redefine yourself and focus on what is truly important, will you not gain renewed sense of purpose and renewed meaning from your performance focused actions? When you assist others in achieving their goals, is that not fulfilling a basic human need and achieving a greater purpose in your life?

The second tier of Maslow's hierarchy of needs is esteem needs. We all have the need for self-esteem, self-respect and the respect / esteem of others. As you practice the

Impact Performance! principles and make progress, you will gain confidence and more self-esteem. You will begin to accomplish more; thus, you will be a success. It is important to realize that no matter where you are in your life, there is room for improved performance in Life's Outcomes. As you develop and live a process for continual personal performance improvement and begin to share these principles with others, you will gain others' respect. They will see the new light you shine, the light that illuminates their path to success.

The third tier is a sense of belonging, love, friendship and appreciation. One of the four key Life Categories is Relationships. You are to measure the ability to manage your relationships for greater good and mutually beneficial outcomes. You will see the importance of relationships and the interconnectivity of your relationship management style to the other Life Categories. When you begin to put your IP!-PIM plan into practice, you will improve your relationship management style and actions. As your relationships begin to improve, you reap the fruits of these interactions and commitments; you will experience the sense of belonging and increase your capacity to meet the success needs and goals of others. You will become more value-added in all relationships you accept.

The forth tier of Maslow's hierarchy of needs is security. These are basic needs such as the security of your family and their future, hunger, shelter, etc. Three of Life's Categories (Health, Career and Finances) play pivotal roles in your confidence to deliver and enjoy security for you and your family. All of us know the importance of living a healthy life, progressing in our careers, and being good stewards of our finances. Yet, we tend to take too much for granted and continue to take actions that are contrary to what we know to be good for our future and us. We will outline a plan of action that will help you to stay focused on that which is truly important and achieve greater security.

The most basic of human needs is, of course, physiological. These needs include that which are required to sustain life such as water, food, shelter, warmth, sleep, etc. We assume you meet physiological needs today.

As humans, we share these basic needs and the desire to meet these needs. The guiding principles presented here are meant to help you meet these basic human needs and to go further than you imagined given your current paradigm of thought and action which has led to sub-optimal performance and outcomes. The intention is of course to better satisfy these needs and advance towards the top of the pyramid.

The reason Maslow's hierarchy is a pyramid is simple. A person is to meet the needs of the bottom level then move upward; it forms a base for upward movement. That is, one must meet the basic Physiological needs first before satisfying the needs of the next higher level, Safety and Security. Then, once the needs of Safety and Security are met one can strive to meet the basic need of Sense of Belonging, and so forth. Maslow recognized that it is difficult or impossible to strive for Self-Actualization if the Security need is unsatisfied, for example.

Is it not interesting that people spend most of their time and energy satisfying Physiological, Safety and Security, and Sense of Belonging needs; yet a large percentage of people struggle to satisfy the human need of Self-Esteem and few achieve Self-Actualization. Why?

You probably have some thoughts regarding how to answer this question. One postulate: we are programmed to meet the lower needs of the pyramid, not to progress further. Early adulthood (i.e. education) is designed to meet Safety and Security needs and create a family life and social structure that satisfies our Sense of Belonging. Some satisfy Self-Esteem needs as they mature, develop mastery, and gain the respect of others. However, is there a given model to satisfy our higher levels of human needs? Most pursue self-gratification that yields a lack of "sense of self." Programming by societal norms and our own patterns of behavior reinforce the need to satisfy only the lower levels of human needs. Elephants keep us from achieving greater satisfaction of Self-Esteem and Self-Actualization needs. Eat the elephant to move up the pyramid. From the top of the pyramid, you spot the elephants easily.

The IP!-PIM is meant to guide you to higher levels of personal performance. As you develop the ability to better manage the Self-System and demonstrate improved performance, the probability of satisfying Self-Esteem and Self-Actualization needs greatly increases. Elephants stand in your way of satisfying higher levels of human needs; eat them and you will position yourself for greater Self-Esteem and Self-Actualization.

Your purpose in life is to serve humanity. Once you eat the elephant, you can live outside yourself and better serve others to improve their lives.

The Impact Performance! Continuum

"Well done is better than well said."

Benjamin Franklin

Every person can find and identify himself or herself along the Impact Performance! Continuum. It is a continuum because our efforts to improve never cease and there is no end point; there is always room for improvement. This continuum reflects the position or status of our Life's Outcomes and overall performance. Where are you, where do you want to be and how big is the gap between the two?

You may not like where you are as you identify with your performance outcomes. This is a motivating response; embrace it. Do not allow identification and definition of your current performance level defeat you! Rather, use this emotional response in helping you to change and achieve your Impact Goals.

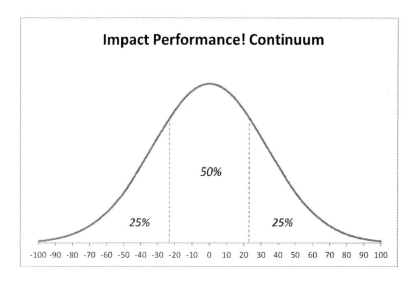

The scale is -100 to 100, which is arbitrary. The use of the Impact Performance! Continuum scale is to assign a value to your performance level. The aim is to quantify performance improvement and to make it a measureable entity.

If you have taken a statistics class, you will recognize this "bell shaped curve" as a normal distribution. Essentially this means that the performance levels (outcomes) of humans are normally distributed (mean = 0, standard deviation = 33.33). Given this assumption, we see that according to this scale, 50% of us fall within the range of performance levels, -22 to 22. One quarter (25%) are below the -22 level and one quarter (25%) are above the +22 level.

Additionally:

- The top 10% are at or above the 43 mark; the bottom 10% are below the -43 mark.
- The top 5% are at or above the 55 mark; the bottom 5% are below the -55 mark.

- Further, the top 1% performs at or above the 78 mark and the bottom 1% performs below the -78 mark.

Overall Impact Performance! is the average of the performance levels across the twelve sub-categories of the four Life Categories: Health, Relationships, Career, and Finances. We will benchmark your performance in each sub-category of the Life Categories and calculate your current overall performance. As you can imagine, we are to advance to greater levels of performance along the Impact Performance! Continuum. Soon you will establish an action plan to achieve improvement. As you progress, you will be able to note your progress on the performance continuum, which provides a visual reinforcement of your improvement. Again, this is a function of progress across all of the Life Categories.

Note if your current performance level is in the negative range, this does not constitute failure (the continuum is a relative scale). Everyone is at a different level of personal performance along this continuum.

You are to become primarily concerned with progress, not where you are today. To be overly concerned with current performance levels (CPL) is a limiting thought pattern, which will hold you back. We use this scale as a means to track progress. If you do fall in the negative range, it simply means there is greater urgency to get moving!

You may quickly see a performance level along the continuum in which you desire (e.g. top 25%, >+22), and say, "I don't know how to achieve that level of performance in life; otherwise I would be there already." This is natural. Remember, you have elephants in your way and are programmed to achieve sub-optimal performance. Now is the time to move forward.

The contention here is that your Power Source combined with Self-Leadership yields your current level of performance. We will change and improve these determinates of performance in order to demonstrate greater and more positive outcomes; i.e. to deliver Impact Performance!

The great news is that you can achieve greater levels of performance by eating the elephant, attaining a performance focus and striving for balance. The IP!-PIM will guide you. Soon you will move forward, see your progress and deliver Impact Performance! Keep going.

Performance Is Reality - Everything Else Is Noise.

Your mission is to progress forward along the Impact Performance Continuum and to live a life of Impact Performance! The IP!-PIM was developed to guide you along the Impact Performance! Continuum.

To solve a problem that appears unsolvable or insurmountable, one must breakdown the problem into smaller more digestible bites. Then, as you consume the smaller bites, the solution to the once "impossible" problem begins to appear. We will use performance continuums for each of the Life Category sub-categories (the smaller bites).

Remember, to eat the elephant, you are to take it one bite at a time. No matter what you are facing, you can overcome and succeed.

Below is the Impact Performance! Personal Improvement Model (IP!-PIM). This is your model for eating the elephant:

IP!-PIM

Bite #1: Embrace the Impact Missions-Values Statement

Bite #2: Envision Impact Performance!

Bite #3: Benchmark Impact Performance! Across the Life Categories

Bite #4: Redefine Success & Set Life Category Goals

Bite #5: Establish the Measurement System

Bite #6: Identify the Elephants

Bite #7: Create the "Eat the Elephant" Action Plan

Get Moving, Live a Life of Impact Performance!

This model provides a stepwise guide to greater levels of performance. By taking these bites, you become performance focused. In Bite #1, you will adopt and embrace the Impact Mission-Values Statement. This becomes your foundation for Self-Leadership. In Bite #2, you will envision the person you want to become and to envision greater Power Source necessary to ignite change. Bite #3 is the act of benchmarking present performance levels in the sub-categories, which yield overall performance. With Bite #4, you will redefine success and acknowledge the Life Category Goals. This Bite clearly establishes the overarching performance focus. You establish performance measures in Bite #5 to track progress. You will establish performance measures for the Power Source, Self-Leadership and the Life Categories. In

Bite #6, you identify your elephants, the obstacles that stand in your way of improvement. You will create an action plan to eat the elephants and establish clear time-based objectives and milestones in Bite #7.

Which is the most important Bite? They are all equally important but most importantly, you must get moving! Even if you savor each Bite, nothing is accomplished until you put your action plan in motion and begin to live a life of Impact Performance! Be the person you envision and make it happen. There is no reason to wait. Get moving today.

For continuous improvement, it is necessary to measure performance on an on-going basis and re-take bites as necessary (action-control). When you reach stated Impact Objectives and milestones toward your overall goals, then you establish new ones and keep moving forward along the Impact Performance! Continuum. Once you eat the elephant, and look for another one to eat, you become a true hunter.

As you might imagine, over time you will need to revisit the Bites and revise your action plan. It is natural that as you eat elephants, others appear and you will have to establish strategies and tactics to continue your journey of personal performance improvement. Remember, there is always room for improvement.

This not a self-help, make you feel better, new age, or philosophical book. Rather, the IP!-PIM is proven to create a process where you can demonstrate measurable progress towards your Impact Goals. It is not enough to say I "feel" better about myself; you need to demonstrate to yourself and to others that you are making progress with tangible results. Once you begin to demonstrate progress, your confidence grows and the ability to manage change will come naturally.

It is highly motivating and reinforcing for you and others to experience your performance improvement. Open yourself up to others and engage them in your quest to eat the elephant.

All of us possess untapped potential to meet our fundamental needs and to help others. An axiom in personal performance improvement is that "You shall reap that which you sow." If you truly dedicate yourself in all aspects of your life, you will become a different and better person given the proper tools, guidance, motivation and on-going support. You can tap greater Power and exert greater Self-Leadership to meet your basic human needs. You have what it takes to achieve Impact Success.

You are to establish a process whereby you can conquer any challenge, any personal elephant; it is a journey not a means to an end. The darkest hours and how we handle challenging situations are defining moments in our lives. The ability to face any obstacle with a positive attitude and not be defeated by any person, place, thing or circumstance will yield greater happiness and contentment in your life. Here is the great news; no matter your current situation, you can improve your performance and your life's outcomes. You can make an Impact!

There are no guarantees in life. We all know the future is not certain. However, you can increase the probability of becoming the person you desire to become by committing to the demonstration of progress towards your goals, striving for balance and by maintaining a performance focus. Your measured progress along the Impact

Performance! Continuum is your demonstration of positive personal improvement and of the person you desire to become.

To be clear, the person most responsible for your success is you. The first step is to declare I will improve my performance.

Since you have a desire to change, now is the time to make the following declaration:

I will not be defeated. I will redefine success and I will be successful. I will live with a performance focus and balance my life. I will demonstrate positive outcomes and help others succeed. I will not sacrifice the gift of life. I will live a life of Impact Performance!

Once you declare a commitment to personal performance improvement, you are on the path of Impact Success. Congratulations! You are an Elephant Eater in the making.

An Elephant Eater is a person who can overcome that which holds them back and takes control of their life; Elephant Eaters demonstrate improved performance across the Life Categories.

Ultimately, Elephant Eaters strive to help others eat the elephant. Those who have proven results as Elephant Eaters can graduate to become Elephant Hunters. The Hunter helps others to adopt the IP!-PIM and lives a life of Impact Performance!

The great news is that no matter where you fall on the Impact Performance! Continuum, you can progress, be successful, live a life full of positive Impact and eventually help others to succeed.

Our hope is that you will pursue Impact Performance! with conviction and diligence.

Get moving and brace for the Impact!

3

The Biggest Elephant

Eat Yourself: Redefine, Analyze, Energize

The biggest elephant is you. "What?!" you say. That is correct; the biggest elephant that stands in your way is you. You allow other elephants to define you and limit your vision. You live a programmed life. You listen to self-limiting talk and poor advice from others who are not committed to your success. You convince yourself you cannot achieve success. Why?

There are many reasons humans allow themselves to "hit a wall," limit their own potential, and even regress. One reason is the convenience of the path of least resistance. It is easier to acquiesce than to accept and overcome challenges in order to grow. It is easier to use the excuse and convenience of programming by societal norms, our upbringing, and the subpar expectations of others, than to face our greatest fears and challenges.

The biggest elephant you face is yourself. You will have to eat the old you and create a new you, the Impact you, the Elephant Eater. Do not look back. The past is gone. There is no value in reliving the past unless to learn from it.

Redefine

Who are you? Who is the person you truly desire to be? Are these two different people? Do not worry as most of us would like to better ourselves; we just do not have the guidance and support to do so.

The Impact Team is asking you to redefine yourself. Now is the time to embrace the thought of being a performance-focused person who eats elephants for breakfast, lunch and dinner. In the next section, you will begin to create the new you, the Elephant Eater.

To change, you will need to improve Self-Leadership management and the ability to tap into your Power Source. This is not as simple as it sounds and most people tend to backslide because they are hesitant, and fearful of the unknown. The best way to make a fundamental change is to do it. That is correct, dive head first without hesitation.

If you get down or even depressed, press forward and maintain your performance focus. Your darkest hours present the greatest opportunity to prove to yourself who you truly are – you are capable of overcoming any obstacle with greater Power and Self-Leadership. The "Impact you" sees challenges as opportunities.

As you ponder this concept, you are to rely on your Impact Vision and the use of visualization techniques to create the vision of a life of Impact. As you focus on the Life Category Goals and eat the identified elephants, the old self-limiting talk and behaviors melt away. Do not identify with what is *wrong* with you, identify with what is *right*!

To eat the "you-Elephant," you will need to change your belief system about yourself and your capabilities (you are more capable of improvement than you currently think). Begin to use positive self-talk constantly. The inner conversation and monologue should always be positive and originate from a point of a problem solver; nothing can defeat you. You can overcome anything, for you are an Elephant Eater!

Analyze

How well do you perform today? How do you know? Measurement is at the heart of Impact Performance! Since the biggest elephant is you, think back on the occasions and missed opportunities to overcome challenges and to help others achieve. Analyze yourself. Take a deep look into how well you perform in the Life Categories: Health, Relationships, Career and Finances.

As you go forward, you will learn the Impact Performance! – Personal Improvement Model and apply its guidelines and principles to your life. You will conduct introspection and take inventory of the person you are; and, you will envision the new you. Performance levels will be benchmarked on a granular level. Soon, you will know where you stand in terms of overall Impact Performance!, in each of the Life Categories and in each of the respective sub-categories. You will identify the #1 elephants across the sub-categories, who may in fact be you. This analysis affords the Elephant Eater a clear picture of what must be done to achieve personal performance improvement and leave the old you behind.

Energize

How do you achieve sustainable positive change and improvement? If you knew exactly what to do, it is ultimately up to you to make it happen. It takes renewed energy and additional Power to leave the sub-optimal you behind and achieve Impact Success.

You have more Power potential than you realize. Channel any doubt or frustration you experience or feel into action. Become an action-oriented and a performance-focused person. Rid yourself of the old you and become the Impact you. Plug into your Power Source and begin living a life of Impact Performance! Stay hungry and get moving!

There are no excuses and no doubts. You can accomplish anything.

4

The Servings:

The Impact Performance! Personal Improvement Model

"If you don't know where you are going, any road will lead you there."

Wizard of Oz

Bite #1: Embrace the IMPACT Mission-Values Statement

Grab a pen and some paper. You will need to take some notes while munching on this first bite.

Your Impact Mission-Values statement is what navigates you in the rough seas of life. It is the foundation from which every thought, spoken word, decision, behavior and action flows.

"My mission is to deliver Impact Performance! in my life and in the lives of others."

Where Impact stands for:

I   **I**ntegrity

M   **M**aking a difference

P   **P**assion for excellence

A   **A**lways improve

C   **C**ompassion for others

T   **T**aking risks

Embrace the Impact Mission-Values statement and your foundation fundamentally changes. Your thoughts, conversations, behaviors and actions stem from IMPACT. This solid foundation helps to establish a performance focus. This is not a bragging rite. Rather, it is a living mission statement. It redefines who you are and the values held with conviction. It is what you do. You will never live a moment of regret if you adhere to the mission and values espoused in the Impact Mission-Values statement.

Every day you have the opportunity to make a positive Impact in your life and in the lives of others; you have a gift. It is within you; live it.

Integrity

Merriam-Webster's definition of integrity:

1. Firm adherence to a code of especially moral or artistic values
2. An unimpaired condition

3. The quality or state of being complete or undivided

Do you know anyone who possesses integrity? If so, you want to emulate them. Integrity is attainable; it is within your grasp. All you have to do is decide to become a person of integrity, a person of good moral character, and a person who is solid and dependable. A person of integrity follows through on his or her commitments. Once you decide to become a person of integrity, do it.

People are not born with integrity; they earn it by demonstration of the personal decisions and actions they take and how they treat others. We all know the golden rule of "Treat others like you want to be treated." This is a golden rule indeed and we can all think twice before we say something or before we act in order to question ourselves, "Is this the right thing to say or do in this situation to ensure a positive outcome for those involved?" To deliver Impact, you must strive to be a person of integrity. Have you noticed that people of integrity are typically unflappable in the face of challenge? People of integrity are the people others turn to when in need. It is simply because people of integrity can be trusted. As such, you should strive to become more dependable and more trustworthy every day. Those who lie, cheat, steal, deceive and take advantage of others are not living a life of IMPACT.

What can you do today to become a more trustworthy and dependable person? If some thoughts popped into your mind, write those action items down.

Making a difference

A life of Impact is about making a positive difference in your life and the lives of others. You may proclaim that you already deliver positive influence. You can do more to effect positive change in others. All you are doing at this point is declaring that you going to do it. As part of your Mission-Values Statement, you are committing to delivering positive outcomes for yourself and for others.

What can you do to make a positive difference in your life and in the lives of others? Can you be a better role model? Write those ideas down.

Passion for excellence

One definition of passion is an intense, driving, or overmastering feeling or conviction and devotion to some activity. The definition of excellence is the quality of being excellent. Elephant Easters are people who have a passion for excellence in every aspect of their life. No matter the situation, you should strive for the highest standard. If you work, then you strive to be the best in your profession and deliver as much value as possible. In your relationships, you strive for the best possible outcomes from the connection with that person; you are to be more value-added in that relationship. You strive for excellence in your overall health and in the management of your finances. In any endeavor or activity you choose, you possess an intense drive to achieve that which you once thought impossible. You strive more and more for mastery in every aspect of your life.

Winston Churchill had a lisp as a child and became one of the greatest orators and leaders in history. Benjamin Franklin was criticized, as a poor writer early in life, then became a prolific writer and leader. There are countless examples of people who took a seemingly insurmountable negative and made it a positive in their life with a passion to excel in that endeavor. Whatever your perceived struggle, recognize it as such and overcome it with a passion for excellence. Remember, if you say you cannot do something, you are probably correct because you believe you cannot. Now, start believing you can! Change the conversation and negative thought patterns such that you believe that anything is possible. Tell yourself that you can achieve and the likelihood of achieving increases by an order of magnitude.

Do you possess passion for something in your life? If so, identify with those feelings and prepare to apply in other areas. Where could you apply more passion for excellence in your life? Jot those areas down.

Always improve

Impact Performance! stems from the concept of continuous improvement - to develop a process that affords on-going improvement in all aspects of life (i.e. the Life Categories). Remember, there is always room for improvement in all things. So as you progress, recall your Mission-Values Statement to "always improve."

Personal performance improvement is the demonstrable attainment of greater levels of performance in all four of the Life Categories. As an elephant eater, you have an insatiable appetite to "always improve."

What are the biggest areas of your life that you perceive need improvement? Write them down.

41

Compassion for others

Compassion is a sympathetic consciousness of others' distress combined with a desire to alleviate that distress. To show compassion is to recognize the distress someone is under and to do something about it. It is not enough to feel bad or sorry for someone for whatever is of distress to them; you must possess a desire to help them to alleviate that distress. You have the capacity to help others. Practice the art of questioning others about their troubles. Offer support in any shape, form or fashion in your capacity to help them overcome. Keep in mind, good deeds will come back to you ten-fold.

Has anyone ever shown you compassion in your time of need? It probably was an overwhelming experience and feeling. You can demonstrate and give this to others - you have it and it is the greatest of selfless gifts. If you are a selfish person, learn to help others. If your focus is inward, then become more outwardly focused. If you are vane, showing compassion for others is not to elevate you. Rather, you help others not for your glory, but because it is the right thing to do. Do not talk about it - simply do it.

Compassion is a learned trait. You can become more compassionate. Seek out opportunities to help others every day. It can be something small, but offer your assistance. Your Impact Mission-Values Statement calls for compassion; help someone today.

What are the ways you can recognize distress in others? Do you offer to help others with their needs? Write down how you recognize distress and directly enhance the lives of others. What are some opportunities to become more compassionate? Make note.

Taking risks

Only those who will risk going too far can possibly find out how far one can go.

T.S. Elliot

Thus far, we have discussed integrity, making a difference, a passion for excellence, to "always improve" and possessing compassion for others. You may feel outside of your comfort zone at this point, which is great because that is where you need to be to create change. Those who live IMPACT are not afraid to take risks and push the envelope. Remember there is great learning opportunity in taking risks. The only way to fail is not to try. Even if you try something and it does work out like you thought, that does not define failure. Edison said of the development of the light bulb after trying thousands of experiments, "I did not fail; I just found 10,000 ways not to do it."

In the world of experimentation, there is a saying, "Be bold, but not crazy." In this context, scientists attempt many ways of testing their theories. However, they do not try something that is unsafe or will yield a high probability of a negative result. You should try new things and push the envelope in your pursuit of living a life of Impact Performance! but nothing too crazy or unsafe, Ok?

There is great reward in taking the risks required to overcome the challenges you face. The greater the challenge is, the greater is the opportunity to demonstrate your ability to overcome that challenge. If you conquer your greatest fear, will it not be easier to conquer anything you face? Take the risk.

You will never know if you can or cannot climb the mountain unless you make the attempt. Always take the first step. Even if the step is not along the best path, learn from the experience to become more knowledgeable of the correct path. Never give up and never surrender. Be bold in your thinking, and bold action follows.

If we always take the easy route, what have we learned? The only true failure is not to try. You are to learn from your mistakes and your experiments. Learn to avoid the actions that yield sub-optimal performance outcomes.

The application of knowledge for positive gain is wisdom.

What are some areas of your life where you would like to take more bold risks and try some new ways of performing? Write down how you can take more risks and push your envelope.

Your Impact Mission-Values Notes

You have now learned the essence of the Impact performance person that stems from the Impact Mission-Values Statement. You were asked to make notes. Do you have some concrete action items? Again, you may be outside your comfort zone and thinking, "How can I do this?" This is natural, not to worry. You have accomplished much at this point. Reflect on your Impact Mission-Values Statement. What does it mean to you? Take some time to digest this bite as it is a big one.

Can you envision a different "you" which operates from a much different level and viewpoint? Spend the time necessary to reflect on your Impact Mission-Values notes. Close your eyes; see yourself as a person of integrity, a person who makes a difference, a person with a passion for excellence, a person who always strives to improve, a compassionate person and a risk taker. This is the IMPACT person; this is you, the Elephant Eater.

If you are ever in doubt about whom you are and what you stand for, it is IMPACT. Lean on your Impact Mission-Values statement when you question yourself, your decisions and when taking your next steps. Elephant Eaters live IMPACT.

Once you make the declaration that you will live a life of Impact Performance!, then you have taken the first bite of the elephant. Congratulations, you are on your way to improved personal performance. Soon you will be able to satisfy your hunger by feasting on those elephants that get in the way and hold you back. They should look a little smaller and more palatable at this point.

Bite #2: Envision Your Impact

"How am I going to live today in order to create the tomorrow I am committed to?"

Anthony Robbins

One of the habits expounded by Steven Covey in his best-selling book, *The Seven Habits of Highly Successful People,* is to keep the end in mind. When you consider the future, you should think and ponder in this context. When you are lying on your deathbed, will you say, "I wish I had watched more television?" I hope that this will not be the case. Instead, you want to look back on a life full of Impact and no regret. If you give your very best each day to improve yourself and the lives of others, you will become very content and satisfied with your life; there will be no regrets. Elephant Eaters become masters of their destiny, not victims of circumstance. Your improvement success is rooted in your belief system. If you believe anything is possible, you open yourself up to possibilities. If you are negative and narrow your vision, then you deny yourself the endless possibilities that truly exist. Remember that the sun is still shining on a cloudy day; opportunities and possibilities exist even when life appears dark and gray. The Impact effort is to increase the probability of achieving your vision for the future.

We are programmed to think and feel a certain way based on our history, our guidance during our formative years, societal norms, and comparing ourselves to others. You have to let go of the past and of superficial comparisons. Break the chains that limit the thinking of who you are and what your future can be. Once you break the cycle of negative thought patterns and self-limiting speech, you can more easily see the light of endless possibility and achievement.

The future is uncertain and not written in stone. Think about it. Can you predict what will happen tomorrow? No. Nevertheless, tomorrow will come; how you perform is up to you. Given your Impact Mission-Values Statement, it is now time to define who you want to become. What is your vision? What kind of person do you see yourself as in the future? What will be your Life's Outcomes? How will you conduct yourself in the face of challenges? When you look back from the future, what will you see? Will it be full of Impact or will it not?

Why are sports teams victorious when they are inferior to the opponent by all measures? They believe they can win. They have a vision of victory that inspires them to overcome the odds of sure defeat (great coaches deliver inspired vision). In our context here, your vision of the future should be inspirational and a motivating force. Visualization is a big bite of the elephant. You can do it.

Colin Powell stated, "Perpetual optimism is a force multiplier." This quote means that if you are optimistic about the outcome of your challenges, you are more likely to succeed. This suggests more than faith alone. It suggests that your belief system is a key determinate in your Life's Outcomes. As you develop your vision for the future, possess perpetual optimism. As such, you are more likely to achieve that vision. There is no room for negativism at the Impact Vision hotel.

How do you develop a vision? First break away from any preconceived notions. You are not destined to be anything other than what you choose to be. Your future is based upon your belief system, your thought patterns, your inner and outer conversations, the decisions you make and your actions. Once you have cleared your mind of negative thoughts about the future, imagine the type of person you wish to become. This may include your station in life such as a career position or as a grandparent, but go deeper in thought. Consider your processes of thought, decision-making, and action. Think of the type of person you want to be. Do you want to meet all of Maslow's hierarchy of needs: self-actualization, esteem, a sense of belonging, and security? Think how you will face challenges. How will you act in the face of adversity? Will you view change as an opportunity? Imagine yourself as a person who can be relied upon, trusted, well respected in all areas of life, a person who is healthy inside and out, a person who is full of passion and a zest for life, and person who helps others succeed. Recall the IMPACT person called for in the Impact Mission-Values Statement; this is an admirable vision.

Ultimately, the vision you develop is yours. The more concrete your Impact vision, the more concrete a plan that can be developed to get you there and increase your probability of achieving that vision.

Now spend ample time visualizing and practicing positive self-talk. As needed, read articles and books on visualization and positive self-speech. Do whatever it takes to create your Impact vision.

As you spend time pondering, eliminate any binding or limiting thought. Remove the phrase "I can't" from your vocabulary and replace it with "I can." Developing a clear vision of who you are to become can take a day or a week; it simply depends on how much garbage you need to dispose of first. A suggestion is to keep your Impact Performance!

Journal handy, so that as positive thoughts of the future pop into your mind, you can capture those and reflect upon them later.

Some authors suggest using meditation techniques to elicit positive visions of the future. If this works for you, then use meditation. For some it may be enough to take a hike in the mountains or simply invest in some well-deserved quiet time to develop your vision. Another positive practice is to spend time with people who you admire and learn more about what makes them "tick." Spending time with people of integrity will help as you formulate your vision.

Now, it is time to write down the characteristics of the person you wish to become. Keep the end in mind as you make your list. This is not a bucket list or a list of the things you wish to accomplish. It is a listing of the traits and characteristics of the Impact person you envision. Write down the person you wish to become now.

My vision of the Impact person I aim to become:

_____

_____

_____

_____

_____

_____

_____

_____

Bite #3: Benchmark Your Performance Across the Life Categories

Today marks the first day of the rest of my life.

Make that which appears unmanageable or insurmountable, manageable and surmountable by breaking down the issue, challenge or problem into smaller more digestible pieces. In this way, you make progress, one bite at a time.

The four Life Categories are broken down into twelve sub-categories. In this way, you focus on the key aspects of the Impact life. Importantly, when we begin to focus on these sub-categories, specific elephants appear. You identify the elephants to eat them, never to appear again.

The act of benchmarking performance affords an examination of where you are today. You need to be honest regarding current performance levels (CPLs) in each of the Life Categories and take stock of yourself before advancing to more tasty bites of the elephant.

Benchmarking yourself is not easy and takes some guts. However, if you truly want to eat an elephant, you have to inventory yourself. Do not think of this in a negative sense, but make it a positive experience. This is a pivotal step to personal performance improvement and you are succeeding.

Actually, this is a fun bite. You get to take a close look at yourself with the realization that you are going to perform at higher levels in the very near future. This is introspection and dimensions your performance on a granular level in each of the twelve respective sub-categories of the Life Categories; i.e. Life Outcomes.

Your ability to improve in each sub-category ultimately drives overall Impact Performance! which is the average of the performance in each of the twelve sub-categories.

Recall the four Life Categories:

- Health
- Relationships
- Career
- Finances

As you go forward, you will dive deep into each of the Life Categories, the interconnectivity between the categories and the importance of balance across each. Keep in mind that all Life Categories are equal in importance. Also, do not worry about how to improve at this point, only focus on your current performance levels.

Now, we will discuss the Life Categories in general terms for benchmarking your current performance level and outcomes.

There is no right or wrong answer here. Marking a value too high or too low does not buy you anything. Just input the value you think reflects your current performance in the given sub-category of the Life Categories.

Health Performance Benchmark

Health Performance is comprised of your mind, body and spirit. Think of these three components of health in terms of strength and agility for your age bracket. It is easy to think of your body in terms of strength and agility but you can measure and improve your mind and spirit in terms of strength and agility as well.

Mental strength and agility refers to your current ability to use both sides of your brain and stay mentally fit (analyze, problem solve; yet create too). It is given, based on scientific research that elderly people who maintain active mental strength and agility stave off the onset of Alzheimer's disease. Presently there is no cure for Alzheimer's disease, but it is believed that the onset can be delayed.

Signs of memory loss typically show in the 40's and 50's but the research indicates that the mentally debilitating disease can begin as early as the 20's. A clear negative is the amount of time a person watches television or performs unchallenging repetitive actions. A clear positive is learning new activities and hobbies that exercise the mind, such as playing the guitar, chess, learning to paint, sculpture, working puzzles, etc. So, as you benchmark your mental health strength and agility, consider whether you are exercising your analytical skills and your creative side as well on an on-going basis. Does your mind respond accurately and quickly when challenged or stimulated?

Your physical strength and agility refers, of course, to your current physical condition. When you think of your present physical performance level, consider the amount and quality of the physical strength you need upon demand. Does your body perform satisfactorily?

We typically do not consider our spirit in terms of our health and overall wellness. However, as above, you can think of your spiritual health in terms of strength and agility. We are not discussing religion here; rather, the context is along the lines of your attitude, disposition, countenance and the sentient part of a person - your emotional side. We will refer to this sub-category of Health Performance as the "emotional" part of overall health. We all know persons who have a positive persona no matter the occasion and we know of persons who always see the negative vs. the positive in any given situation. We know those who "blow their top" or "lose it" often vs. those who remain calm and who have an even temperament. Some have greater and some have lesser spirit strength and agility (i.e. emotional performance levels).

It is within your purview to juxtapose a positive disposition given any situation. That is a mouthful. The point is that you can control your emotions to achieve a better outcome. What is your spirit or emotional performance level? When faced with a negative stimulus, do you fall apart easily or do you maintain composure? Are you unflappable? The great news is that you can improve your spirit / emotional performance in any given circumstance or situation.

Recall The Impact Performance! Continuum where performance was normally distributed. We will make the same assumption in the case of Health Performance. Some could easily argue that the Health Performance distribution is skewed to the lower side of the scale due to increasingly poor behavioral choices (high fat diet, lack of sleep, vices, increasing stressors, inability to cope, etc.). The aim of this exercise is to benchmark your sub-categories of Health Performance. We are to find values along this continuum that reflect the performance of your mind, body and spirit performance.

To calculate your current Health Performance level, you are to average the sub-category performance levels of mind, body, and spirit, which are the mental, physical, and emotional performance levels.

Body, Physical

Your body performance benchmark refers to your current physical output.

You may think, "Should I benchmark my body mass index, blood pressure, or heart rate?" At this point, it will suffice to mark where you *think* you are in terms of the performance of your body when you need it to respond to positive and negative stimuli.

For example, if you participate in a sporting event, take a hike with a friend, go for a walk, etc., does your body respond and perform to your satisfaction? As you are scoring your body's performance, consider your energy level too. Are you satisfied with your natural energy level (not drug induced from caffeine or other sources)? Is the energy available when you want it and in the quantity you desire?

Are you in the worst, below average, average, above average, or best physical condition? Give yourself a score between -100 and 100 to reflect your current physical performance. Recall 50% of us will be in the range of -22 to 22 on the performance scales. For example, let us say you believe you are "out of shape" and you have "lost a step" in doing the activities you used to enjoy so much. You have a "not so good" body mass index (high percent body fat) and you may have high blood pressure, etc. Further, your energy level is down and your sex life is not what it used to be. You know you could do better, but you "don't have time to work-out." In this scenario, you are in the negative range of -30 to -40. On the other hand, if you are highly active (e.g.

jog every day), eat very healthy, sleep well, have no physical vices, have normal cholesterol levels, and your energy is very high, then you are likely in the +30 to +40 range. Recall, the top 10% are 43 or above and the bottom 10% of body performance is -43 or below.

Score your Physical Performance and note here: _____

For most, the focus will be solely on the body sub-category of Health Performance. We need to avoid this tendency and remember to consider the Health Performance sub-categories of the mental and emotional as well.

Mind, Mental

The mind is highly complex. We are not here to disect it or over-analyze the mental state; we are only concerned with mental performance as a sub-component of overall Health Performance.

As most of us are aware, we possess untapped mental capacity. We have the capacity to learn something new every moment of every day. It is vitally important to keep our minds sharp; that is, both sides of the brain active - the analytical and the creative. We must challenge our minds constantly to keep them sharp. Suffice it at this point to simply note where you *think* you are in terms of mental strength and agility.

Are you in the worst, below average, average, above average, or best mental condition? For example, can you easily recall what you ate for breakfast yesterday or two days ago? Do you often lose your train of thought? Do you "max out" or "burn out" in terms of mental capacity? Are you able to visualize the future easily? Is it difficult to image your future vividly and the path forward? If so, you may be in the negative range. Now on the other hand if your mental performance is sharp, you are able to calculate and articulate well at any given time, you have creative hobbies, and you use both sides of your brain (both analytical and creative), then you are likely in the positive range. Recall that the performance scales are relative in nature. Therefore, there is not a right or a wrong answer. Again, recall 50% will fall in between -22 and 22 in terms of Mental Performance.

Give yourself a score between -100 and 100 to reflect your current Mental Performance.

Score your Mental Performance and note here: _____

Spirit, Emotional

Again, when we speak of "spirit," we do not refer to a religious context. We are refering to a person's persona, countenance, attitude, or sentient side. That is, the emotional side.

There are on-line emotional IQ tests which I do not recommend for benchmarking. You see the idea here is to benchmark what you believe and *think* of your Health Performance sub-categories. This is somewhat subjective, which is what you desire at this point.

Now in terms of emotional performance, let's think again in terms of strength and agility. Are you capable of invoking the correct type and level of emotion needed for any given situation or stimuli? You may not be aware but you have control of your emotions. It is possible to become masters of our thoughts, self-talk, spoken words and emotional performance.

Emotions are on the inside and shown on the outside; the outside emotions are what others see. There are "good" and "bad" emotions and levels therein which you demonstrate. We have all seen emotional outbursts that invariably create a negative experience for everyone involved. On the other hand, we have experienced positive emotions that create positive outcomes for ourselves and those involved.

Are you generating the correct type and amount of emotion on the inside and outside? Are you solving problems or creating them with your emotional performance?

The exercise here is to examine where you are in terms of emotional performance. Note, we are not suggesting one should never express themselves emotionally. Often it is refreshing to "let it out" with a trusted person. It is appropriate to have emotions and express them in the proper context and situation. This benchmarking exercise is to gauge your ability to control how the amplitude of emotional expression and the emotion itself are expressed to yield a positive outcome.

If you explode and have emotional outbursts on a frequent basis (e.g. raise your voice once a week or more) that causes a negative environment, then you are likely in the negative range. If your emotional performance is such that you can control your emotions to achieve a desired state and you are unflappable in a confrontation, can resolve negative situations, and "keep your cool," then you are likely in the positive range.

Are you in the worst, below average, average, above average, or best range in Emotional Performance?

Give yourself a score between -100 and 100 to reflect your current Emotional Performance.

Score your Emotional Performance and note here: _____

Remember that the mind, body, and spirit work together; they are interconnected. If you believe you need to work on one of these sub-categories because it scored lower than the other two, do not forget the other two components of Health Performance. For example, if you believe you need to improve Emotional Performance, that simply means you have developed awareness. Nevertheless, do not let up on your efforts to strengthen your Physical and Mental Performance as those components help to lift the Emotional component of Health Performance due to interconnectivity. Remember to strive for balance.

Congratulations, you have one of the key benchmarks complete. Let us continue this Bite with our Relationship Performance Benchmark.

Relationships Performance Benchmark

"Meaningful partnership with another person requires clearly defined expectations and deadlines; align your actions to meet those commitments. There are no excuses; relationship performance is reality."

How we manage relationships can be a source of great joy or great stress in our lives. The great news is that we can improve our relationship management style and relationship outcomes. As you benchmark your Relationships Performance, keep the following in mind. Do you have long-term trusting relationships? Do you garner respect? Do you establish clear expectations? Do you meet the expectations of others? Do they meet your expectations? Do you have a conscious and expressive relationship management style and activity plan to meet each other's expectations? Do all of your relationships yield positive outcomes? Do you strengthen others? Do they strengthen you? Do you possess the courage to manage a relationship more effectively with a person who creates negative outcomes?

If you answered "no" to any of the above, then of course, there is room for Relationships Performance improvement.

Importantly, in all relationships there is a basic question, "Am I an asset or a liability?" In turn, those with whom you have a relationship are either an asset or liability to you. You may think that sounds selfish to think in these terms. However, the question of asset or liability is born of the desire to quantify your Relationship Performance. You are value-added to the relationship, and, in turn, the other person is value-added to you on an ongoing basis or not. Value equals benefits minus cost. Do you create more benefits to your relationships or create more costs? Do you solve more problems or create more problems in your relationships?

Again, we are attempting to quantify our personal performance, which may be a new concept, especially in terms of relationships. This may seem uncomfortable but press forward as this is a critical Bite of the elephant.

We will benchmark your Relationship Performance by examining performance in the following sub-categories: Work, Family, Friends, and Significant Other.

The key to enduring and trusting relationships is of course, efficient and effective communications to level-set and meet expectations on a going basis. Frustration sets-in when one or both persons in the relationship feel as though their expectations are not a priority. Frustration can lead to resentment and ultimately the demise of the relationship. Frustration is mitigated through effective communication of each other's expectations and in each other's actions to meet those expectations. Often we must adjust expectations based upon the other person's willingness and ability to meet our high expectations. Remember, no one is a mind reader; you must communicate your expectations clearly for those expectations to be satisfied. You own 50% of every relationship you accept.

Therefore, as you are benchmarking the sub-categories of Relationship Performance, also consider your communicative performance. Are you communicating expectations properly?

Relationship Performance refers to your ability to produce mutually beneficial outcomes for all parties involved. Ongoing mutually beneficial outcomes define "great" relationships. You establish your Relationship Performance sub-category benchmarks by this standard.

As with the other performance continuums, we assume Relationship Performance is normally distributed. The average of the sub-category benchmarks constitutes the overall Relationship Performance benchmark.

Our focus now is simply on benchmarking current Relationship Performance levels in the following sub-categories: Work, Family, Friend and Significant Other.

Work Relationship Performance

Work related relationships are complicated by the politicized nature of our corporate cultures, our need to please our superiors, extrinsic motivators, sexual tensions, power struggles, etc. This does not mean it is impossible to develop effective and efficient relationship management models. It simply means we must be more conscious and aware of our environment and the consequences of our communication style and of our actions.

Some are masters in the workplace in establishing clear expectations and reaching mutually beneficial outcomes in nearly every instance, project, or situation. On the other hand, some in the workplace never clearly articulate expectations so it is impossible to meet that which is unknown, thus yielding poor Work Relationship results. It is hard to hit a moving target; no one has a crystal ball or is a mind reader. Remember, effective and efficient communication is the key when establishing expectations.

Keeping in mind that relationships are two-way streets. We have to bear the burden often when the other party does not clearly establish expectations; recall, we own 50% of every relationship we accept. Are you performing well in every work relationship to create mutually beneficial outcomes on an on-going basis (even when the boss is not clear with his or her expectations)?

This is not a measure of your rank or popularity in the work place. Rather, it is what you *think* is your benchmarked performance in terms of establishing clear expectations, and meeting those mutually established expectations. Importantly, if your expectations are not met or you do not deliver upon a given expectation, do you resolve to everyone's satisfaction in a timely manner?

Do you manage work relationships for mutually beneficial gain?

Now, are you in the worst, below average, average, above average, or best range in your Work Relationship Performance?

Give yourself a score between -100 and 100 to reflect your current Work Relationship Performance.

Score your Work Relationship Performance and note here:

_____

Family Relationship Performance

Every topic in this book is touchy because it is about personal performance, but nothing can be more explosive than family relationships. However, whatever the volatility case may be, you must focus on family relationships as a sub-category of Relationship Performance. We do not choose our families, but we can control the influence family relationships have on our Self-System (Power Source, Self-Leadership, and Life's Outcomes).

Family Relationship Performance is a function of your ability to establish mutually beneficial expectations and to deliver upon those expectations in all family relationships (mother-daughter, father-son, mother-son, father-daughter, between siblings, etc.). In addition, Family Relationship Performance is the degree to which you can control the influence of family members on your Life's Outcomes.

Are you close to your extended family members or distant? Do you argue constantly, often, sometimes, occasionally, seldom, or never? Is it impossible to relate to family members or easy? Do you spend time with family out of obligation or love? Are you an asset or a liability in your family relationships? Do you strengthen family members? Do they strengthen you? Whatever the case may be, what do you *think* is your Family Relationship Performance?

Do you manage family relationships for mutually beneficial gain?

Are you the worst, below average, average, above average, or best in your Family Relationship Performance?

Give yourself a score between -100 and 100 to reflect your current Family Relationship Performance.

Score your Family Relationship Performance level and note here: _____

Friend (and former friend) Relationship Performance

We choose our friends. We all realize our friends play pivotal roles in our lives. We listen to our friends; we trust them. They give us advice. We try to please them and we take their advice. Friendships can be a great source of comfort in our time of need. "A friend in need is a friend indeed."

However, our friends can lead us astray. Too often, people who exhibit "bad" behaviors seek out others who enable that behavior as a justification for their own behavior. We are all familiar with peer pressure. People tend to associate with others of a like-mind. "Birds of a feather flock together." Do you enable bad behavior or decry it? Do you engage in gossip or curtail it? Do you lead your friends to positive outcomes or follow others to negative outcomes?

We have all types of friends in our lives. Some friends are closer to us and influence our thoughts, beliefs, decisions, behaviors and actions more than others influence us. Your ability to establish and manage boundaries, i.e. your friend's influence on your Self-System for mutually beneficial positive gain, establishes Friend Relationship Performance.

Our ability to say "no" establishes boundaries in our relationships. It is difficult for some to establish boundaries due to the need for social acceptance. People tend to "go along" with a given behavior even though it produces negative outcomes. Again, it is critical to communicate effectively and efficiently with our friends to create mutually beneficial outcomes.

You may ask, "What about a former friend, former lover, or ex-spouse? How do I best manage Relationship Performance in those circumstances?" Indeed former friends can be a source of irritation and can consume your energy if you allow that to happen. The Relationship Performance principle of putting people in their place with clear boundaries is to be applied to former friends. No matter the reason for the falling-out, your ability to control their influence on you is critical. If former friends remain in your life (e.g. the raising of children from a divorce or within a circle of friends), then your ability to manage those relationships to positive outcomes applies to your Friend Relationship benchmark. How do you handle former friend relationships?

The Power and Self-Leadership to positively influence and lead others (e.g. friends) to positive outcomes is admirable and what you should strive for in improving Relationship Performance. Now, we are simply benchmarking Friend Relationship Performance.

If you accept and allow friends to influence you in a negative way, which produces negative outcomes, then you are in the negative range for Friend Relationship Performance. On the other hand, if you seek and only accept relationships that produce positive outcomes and have friends who are wise, then you are in the positive range.

Do you manage friend relationships for mutually beneficial gain?

Are you the worst, below average, average, above average, or best in your Friend Relationship Performance?

Give yourself a score between -100 and 100 to reflect your current Friend Relationship Performance.

Score your Friend Relationship Performance level and note here: _____

Significant Other Relationship Performance

Couplism is the eating of the elephant, improving performance in each of Life's Categories, and striving for balance together as a couple. There is nothing more sacred (in a secular context) than your relationship with your significant other. Your significant other should be your best friend, your confidant, and your counsel. No other relationship is more critical to your personal performance.

Those who practice Couplism experience an entity that is greater than the sum of the two individuals apart; they are synergistic together. They share life as one, not two people simply co-existing on separate paths of life. Rather, they have the same goals and plans to reach those goals as a single entity. When one suffers, the other suffers as well; when one elates, the other shares in that elation. Those who communicate effectively and efficiently to establish clear and achievable expectations promote the growth in strength / agility of their partnership and increase the probability of ongoing Significant Other Relationship Performance improvement. Those who demonstrate the consistent achievement of those expectations and grow together as one with clear results are living Couplism.

Couplism is achievable. Yes, we are considering love, but we all know couples who were in love, but failed in their relationship. Couplism is the management of the Significant Other relationship for mutually beneficial gain. Are you practicing Couplism daily?

To benchmark your level of Couplism, think of how you perform as a team. Is there synergy? Do you share the same dreams? Are you best friends? Do you confide in others instead of your Significant Other? Do you say positive or negative things about your Significant Other? Are you there for them when they are down? Do you lift them up? Do you do or say anything that you would not do or say in their presence? Do you communicate daily to establish clear expectations and meet those expectations consistently? Are you an asset or a liability to the relationship? Do you strengthen your partner? Do they strengthen you?

In Dr. Gary Chapman's book entitled *The Five Love Languages,* he shows us that couples typically express love in different ways. He demonstrates how we can better express love in ways that our significant other understands. As you consider your Significant Other Relationship performance, think about how you express love and is your love expressed in the most appropriate manner for your partner to receive it.

If not presently in a committed relationship with a Significant Other, then the benchmarking of this sub-category of Relationship Performance is a function of how well you avail yourself to the ideals of Couplism. Perhaps you have been unjustly wronged or hurt by another to the point you feel you can no longer trust anyone? Perhaps you have such an inferiority complex that you believe no other person would want you (a self-defeatist programming)? Perhaps you are so engrossed in your work that you feel as though you cannot allow someone close to you (an imbalance)? Whatever the case may be, benchmark your level of availability and acceptance of the concept and ideals of Couplism.

Do you manage your Significant Other relationship for mutually beneficial gain?

Are you the worst, below average, average, above average, or best in your Significant Other Relationship Performance?

Give yourself a score between -100 and 100 to reflect your current Significant Other Relationship Performance.

Score your Significant Other Relationship Performance and note here: _____

Great job! You have made significant progress thus far in establishing performance benchmarks. Relationships are truly important. How you manage the relationships you accept going forward will dictate much of the joy or stress you experience the rest of your life.

Career Performance Benchmark

When we discuss Career Performance, we are not just talking about your job, we are discussing your long-term ability to satisfy your station in life. All of us should be so fortunate as to find a position matched perfectly with our passion in life. However, it is possible to find passion in your ability to deliver more value in your current occupation.

When benchmarking your Career Performance, do not treat this exercise as an opportunity to "beat yourself up" if you are not where you want to be now or are unhappy with some of your decisions regarding your career moves. Rather, focus on your ability to bring value to the workplace and your passion for what you do in terms of productive time and effort. It is not the amount of income you make that is of interest here, but your level of contentment with how you spend your time. Are you passionate about your work? Are you challenged by your occupation in order to grow professionally?

You spend approximately 45% of your waking hours at work, prepping for work, or in route to work. Moreover, when you meet someone for the first time, one of the first questions is, "What do you do?" As such, you should be excited and enthusiastic about your work. For those whose work misery index is high, their negative feelings about work spill over into the home life and can lead to devastating consequences (recall that all Life Categories are interconnected). Dissatisfaction with Career Performance is a contributing factor for low Relationship Performance, i.e. divorce, for example.

Are you excited to go to work or is it a negative experience? If you are presently unemployed and looking for work, then you are in a tough spot; obviously, we empathize. Your benchmarked Career Performance scores will likely be low, but keep in mind the value you bring to potential employers as you complete this exercise.

We are simply benchmarking now. We will discuss Career Performance in more depth later.

Career Performance is broken down into two sub-categories: Challenge and Passion.

Career Challenge Performance

Career Challenge benchmarking requires you to identify with the level of professional challenge presented by your current position, which affords professional growth. To overcome a challenge in any aspect of life equates to personal growth. When challenged at your work, it presents an opportunity for professional growth. You should pursue additional challenge for ongoing growth. If the opportunity does not present itself, then create more challenge so you can continue to grow and develop greater skill levels and mastery in your work.

If you feel as though your current position is not challenging, dead-end, pigeonholed, or even boring given your level of academic training or ambition, then you will likely score this sub-category in the negative range. However, if you are challenged, ask for more assignments. If ambitions are being met, and you are progressing well in your career with opportunities to advance, then you are in the positive range of Career Challenge Performance.

If you are presently unemployed or seeking a new position, think in terms of the positions you desire. Are your actions geared towards a more challenging role than before? Are you doing the activities needed to advance your career (i.e. networking)?

Are you the worst, below average, average, above average, or best in your Career Challenge Performance?

Give yourself a score between -100 and 100 to reflect your current Career Challenge Performance.

Score your Career Challenge Performance and note here:

_____

Career Passion Performance

Your Career Passion Performance refers to the excitement level associated with your position. Are you valued? Do you feel valued? Is your work recognized and praised? Do you believe in the product or service and the purpose of your company?

If your work misery index is high, then your level of passion is low. If you are not energized and typically late for work or have a high rate of absenteeism, then your Career Passion Performance is likely in the negative range. However, if you are "fired-up" to go to work, giving it your very best in every way, and excited about the value your product and service delivers to customers, then your Career Passion Performance level is probably in the positive range. If you are praised and recognized for your work, feel a sense of accomplishment, and are value-added, then you likely have a have high Career Passion Performance level.

Consider where your passions lie if you are presently unemployed or seeking a new position. Are you pursuing a position with a company who provides products and services for which you have passion?

Are you the worst, below average, average, above average, or best in your Career Passion Performance?

Give yourself a score between -100 and 100 to reflect your current Career Passion Performance.

Score your Career Passion Performance and note here: _____

Finances Performance Benchmark

Your Finances Performance can yield a great sense of security for your family or can be a great source of stress. Your Finances Performance management principles are especially important in regards to how your children eventually manage financial matters (they will emulate your money management patterns). Recall that financial stress and conflicting spending habits are primary attributable causes for divorce. We must become good stewards of our finances; else, we become trapped in financial bondage.

Finances Performance is not whether you live in a large house or a small house; it is not whether you take expensive vacations or not; and it is not about how much money you have in the bank relative to someone else either. Finances Performance is about making the most of what you have for the right reasons.

When benchmarking your Finances Performance, think in terms of wealth creation and your decision-making paradigm in your ability to generate income, when making a purchase and making an investment. Are you too impulsive? Do you have a positive net worth? Do you have a budget? Do you adhere to its guidelines? Do you have multiple streams of income? Do you give to charities?

You may be thinking should I benchmark my credit score, savings rate, or calculate my net worth for this exercise? Now, we are only concerned with how you perceive your personal Finances Performance.

Finances Performance is broken down into the following sub-categories: Income, Spending, and Investing.

Finances Income Performance

When we speak of Finances Income Performance, we are referring to your ability to create income or revenue streams which match the value you bring to the marketplace. For the vast majority, there is one source of income - that is, their employment. For couples, there may be two sources of income - one from each partner. A tenet of Impact Performance! is to seek multiple streams of income. With multiple streams, if one stream were to dry-up for instance, then you have other revenue streams to satisfy your family's needs.

Imagine you lived in a barter system where you had to bring something to the market in exchange to receive the goods and services you desired. What are you bringing to the marketplace and are you generating the level of income you deserve or expect? Are you satisfied with the level of revenue you generate based upon your talents and the value you deliver?

If your level of income is low compared to the value you bring or below expectations, you are likely in the negative range for Income Performance. However, if you have multiple streams of income and generate the income that is equivalent to your delivered value, then you are likely in the positive range.

Are you the worst, below average, average, above average, or best in your Finances Income Performance?

Give yourself a score between -100 and 100 to reflect your current Finances Income Performance.

Score your Finances Income Performance and note here:
_____

Finances Spending Performance

Spending is another touchy subject because it is so emotionally charged. Every purchase decision is based on emotion. We like to think we are objective in our spending but in the final analysis, purchases are emotionally driven. The key concept here is to spend far less than your revenue stream, to create a surplus of funds. Additionally, Finances Spending Performance is adhering to a spending budget and making purchases based on needs vs. wants. There is a tendency to justify everything in our lives, but we must be honest when it comes to Finances Spending Performance.

If you use credit cards regularly and carry credit card debt, live paycheck to paycheck, have a negative cash flow, do not have a budget, and worry everyday about finances (e.g.

paying bills), then you are in the negative range for Finances Spending Performance. If you are an impulse purchaser, and do not get the full use of your purchases (wasteful purchases), then you are in the negative range. However, if you adhere to a strict budget, spend far less than your revenue stream (live below your means), and do not make unwise purchases, you are in the positive range. If you are frugal in your spending, do not use credit cards, and never make an impulse purchase, then you are likely high on Finances Spending Performance scale.

Are you the worst, below average, average, above average, or best in your Finances Spending Performance?

Give yourself a score between -100 and 100 to reflect your current Finances Spending Performance.

Score your Finances Spending Performance and note here:

_____

Finances Investing Performance

Finances Investing Performance is, of course, interconnected to your Finances Income and Spending Performance. If you spend more than your revenue, then you have deficit spending, which is unsustainable. However if you have a surplus of revenue, then you should invest and invest wisely. Finances Investing Performance can be a source of great comfort as you plan for your retirement and family's security. Of course, poor Finances Investing Performance can add additional stress to your Self-System. The disclaimer here is that we cannot offer investing advice per se' but can offer general guidelines.

The premise of Finances Investing Performance is to eliminate debt and create a diversified investment portfolio with the intent of wealth creation. We are not advocating greed here; rather the intent is to reduce liabilities and increase assets to improve your net worth. As shown below:

Net Worth = Assets – Liabilities

The greatest liability for most people who carry debt is credit card debt (due to the very high interest rates). Another form of "bad debt" is the vehicle you drive which is a depreciating asset, meaning it goes down in value over time. If you took a high-risk mortgage and presently you owe more than the property is worth on the open market, then, of course, that mortgage is a liability vs. an asset.

Assets would include the funds you have invested in retirement accounts, savings accounts and cash on hand, equity in your home or business, etc. The idea is to increase your assets while reducing your liabilities to create a positive net worth and to increase your net worth over time. Ultimately, you strive for financial freedom and the ability to help others (e.g. job creation and charitable giving).

If you have a negative net worth, carry significant amounts of credit card debt, and your mortgage loan is greater than the home's value, then you are in the negative range for Finances Investing Performance. If, on the other hand, you have a positive net worth, are creating wealth on an on-going basis, carry minimal debt and have equity in your home, then you are in the positive range for Finances Investing Performance. If you are creating wealth and putting those funds to good use such as creating jobs or giving to charities, then you are high on the Finances Investing Performance Continuum.

Are you the worst, below average, average, above average, or best in your Financial Investing Performance?

Give yourself a score between -100 and 100 to reflect your current Finances Investing Performance.

Score your Finances Investing Performance and note here: _____

Great! Now you have benchmarked performance in the twelve sub-categories of the Life Categories. Now you can calculate your average performance in the Life Categories and your overall Impact Performance! level.

Benchmarked Life Category Performance Levels

Now, simply average your sub-category performance levels in each of the Life Categories to achieve your benchmarked Life Category performance level. List the sub-category benchmarks from above and then take the average:

Health Performance

Physical _____

Mental _____

Emotional _____

Average Health Performance = _____

Relationships Performance

Work _____

Family _____

Friend _____

Significant Other _____

Average Relationships Performance = _____

Career Performance

Challenge _____

Passion _____

Average Career Performance = _____

Finances Performance

Income _____

Spending _____

Investing _____

Average Finances Performance = _____

Awesome! You now have a picture of your current Impact Performance! in each of the Life Categories. These benchmarked levels of performance become important later as we establish our near-term performance improvement milestones in Bite #7.

Your Benchmarked Overall Impact Performance! Level

Next, you will calculate your overall Impact Performance! You are to average the values you noted in each of the Life Category sub-categories above to derive what you believe is your current overall Impact Performance! (the output of your Self-System).

From your notes above, enter the values in the table below. Here is the listing of the 12 sub-categories:

<u>Health Performance Scores</u>

Body, Physical   _____

Mind, Mental   _____

Spirit, Emotional   _____

<u>Relationships Performance Scores</u>

Work   _____

Family   _____

Friends   _____

Other   _____

<u>Career Performance Scores</u>

Challenge   _____

Passion   _____

Finances Performance Scores

Income   _____

Spending   _____

Investing   _____

Now add up all the scores and divide by twelve. Even if a sub-category number is negative, just add up all the numbers and divide by twelve to obtain the average. This is your current Impact Performance! Enter that value here and note the date:

Impact Performance! _____   Date: _____

A quick glance will give you an idea of the sub-categories in which you believe you are performing better vs. other sub-categories. There may be low performance in specific sub-categories in which to concentrate and may be of some urgency, but they are all equally important in the context of Impact Performance! improvement.

Try not to fixate on these values and do not reinforce any negative thoughts because of this exercise. Benchmarking yields a starting point. Your performance today is a benchmark and is relative to future performance levels.

Benchmarking the Power Source

Recall the earlier discussion of the Self-System. To improve outcomes, the input to the system and the process itself would have to change for the better. Further, the mechanism for monitoring change is the measurement system. We will discuss the measurement system in Bite #5. Our present challenge is to benchmark the status of our ability to tap into our source of Power (control the input to the system) and to exert greater Self-Leadership (control the process).

The components of your Power Source are:

- Energy
- Desire, the will to succeed
- Intrinsic self-motivation
- Courage

As you probably imagined, these components are on a continuum just as the performance in each of the sub-categories of the Life Categories. For example, the level of desire and will to succeed is not on or off - the quantity varies. Some have more than others do. The amount of energy varies as well. Do you have the ability to draw upon your well of energy at any given time or any situation? Can you turn up the volume on your intrinsic self-motivation to accomplish that which you desire, or do you tend to give up too easily? It is said that a man of honor and courage will die only one death, but a coward dies many times. Do you have the ability to summon the courage to eat the elephant, or do you cower to the elephants?

Here, we are only concerned with what you *think* is your conscious ability to summon these components of your Power Source as needed in the face of adversity. Remember if you are on vacation, it does not take much courage. However, to improve your life and the lives of others, it will take all components of the Power Source to fuel your Self-Leadership and eat the elephants that stand in your way.

Now benchmark your ability to tap into your Power Source on command.

Are you the worst, below average, average, above average, or best in your ability to tap your Power Source?

Give yourself a score between -100 and 100 to reflect your current Power Source Performance.

Score your Power Source Performance and note here:

_____

Benchmarking Self-Leadership

The components of Self-Leadership are:

- Thought patterns
- Decision making paradigm
- Behaviors
- Actions

Yes, you might have guessed as much, your ability to control your Self-Leadership is on a continuum. There are varying degrees of conscious control over thought patterns (negative to positive), decision making (to increase the probability of a positive outcome), and behaviors and actions leading to your Life Outcomes across the four Life Categories.

We have all seen or know someone whose life is out of control or unstable. The term self-control does not capture the essence of the process we use to produce Life Outcomes or outputs; no, the better description is Self-Leadership. Who is most responsible for your success and progress towards the goals in life? It is you. You are the leader of your life and the person accountable for your outcomes. There is no person, place, thing or circumstance to blame; there are no excuses. Performance is reality.

This may seem harsh, but it is the truth. For you to live a life of Impact Performance! and help others to succeed, you must take Self-Leadership seriously. The great news is that you can actuate more effective and efficient Self-Leadership; it is within you, and it is free.

We will discuss the "how to" later, but for now let us benchmark your ability to consciously control your thought patterns, adjust your decision-making paradigm, and exhibit the most appropriate behaviors (including your spoken words) and actions that yield positive outcomes.

Now benchmark your ability to manage your Self-Leadership on command.

Are you the worst, below average, average, above average, or best in your ability to control and manage your Self-Leadership?

Give yourself a score between -100 and 100 to reflect your current Self-Leadership Performance.

Score your Self-Leadership Performance and note here:

_____

The Impact Team congratulates you. You have taken three bites of the elephant:

1. Your Impact Mission-Values Statement
2. Your Impact Vision
3. Benchmarking Your Life Category Performance

Take a moment to reflect on your progress. You have broken down your life into a system and analyzed the input

(Power Source), the process (Self-Leadership) and the system's output (Life Categories). You have benchmarked the twelve sub-categories that comprise the four Life Categories and calculated your benchmarked performance in each Life Category and your overall Impact Performance! In addition, you have benchmarked your ability to tap into your Power Source on command and your ability to manage Self-Leadership.

From this point forward, you are on a path of Impact Performance! improvement. The simple act of the first three Bites constitutes a path of success; you should feel very positive at this point.

The following Bites of the Impact Performance! - Personal Improvement Model are designed to instill a performance focus, identify your elephants and to detail your action plan.

The first bites are tough and chewy, but once you digest these, you will feel more confident and later bites will be tastier. Stay hungry.

Bite #4: Redefine Success and Set Life Category Goals

"There are no secrets to success. It is the result of preparation, hard work and learning from failure."

Colin Powell (former Chairman of the
U.S. Joint Chiefs of Staff)

Unfortunately, "success" in our culture is defined too greatly by consumerism, individualism, materialism, surface-ism, and by what other people think of us. Surface-ism is an unfortunate but all too real condition we suffer where the outside (i.e. surface) is more important than the inside. The effects of surface-ism can be devastating. Have you ever seen a person spend thousands of dollars on their appearance to improve the "surface" and not a dime improving who they truly are or what they stand for, "the inside"? What if you won the lottery and purchased a big house, a sports car, etc.? Would that fundamentally change you into a better person? No. Of course, money is not a source of happiness, contentment, or satisfaction. Studies show that lottery winners typically become more miserable vs. happier because of their "winning." What have they truly won? The surface is not a true source of happiness.

If you view your life and those around you only for surface-ism, monetary gain or instant gratification, then your life is hollow and without real purpose. Are you vane? If yes, then now is the time to invert from an inward focus to an outward focus. Surface-ism begets more "surface," not depth. Allow your demonstrated performance to reflect who you are as a whole person, not the surface.

Seek the depths of yourself and the depths of others to find peace and life's joy of happiness.

If you succumb to surface-ism, that the appearance of your house and not the home inside defines personal success; then, you are sure to fail by that very measure, as there is never enough. Someone always will have more "surface" than you will. Somehow our culture idolizes youth vs. wisdom; suggests bigger is better, taller is better, a title means something, and prettier is better; a five dollar cup of coffee suggests a higher status; the car we drive symbolizes success, that debt is good etc., etc. We must change our belief system to realize Impact Performance!

Impact Performance! defines success not by societal norms, or in comparison to others. If you allow your Self-Leadership to determine self-worth and self-esteem in comparison to others or by current cultural norms, you will always feel inferior and "bad" about yourself, as there is always someone with a greater degree of surface-ism. That is, someone else will always be prettier, have more money, a bigger house, a more attractive spouse, more power, etc. Material quantity is not above quality characteristics in valuing a person.

We shall redefine success. We are to focus on substance over surface when considering who we are and what success truly means.

Impact Success is defined by demonstrated improvement in each of the Life Categories, a performance focus and striving for balance. Successful Elephant Eaters:

- Live the Impact Vision-Values Statement,
- Engage the Power Source,
- Manage Self-Leadership,

- Strive to achieve Life Category Goals,
- Strive for Balance,
- Measure Impact Performance! for on-going improvement, and
- Help others succeed.

If you pursue the above with commitment and vigor, you are a success by Impact standards. You are on the path now of on-going success and are recognized as such. Feel great about your efforts thus far.

We are defined by our Life Outcomes, how we face challenges (i.e. elephants), and by our demonstrated ability to eat the elephant. Since you have already taken three bites of the elephant, you are on your way to becoming a true Elephant Eater success story.

The degree of realized Impact Success increases as you eat the elephant. Once you have eaten the first, the second becomes easier, the third even easier, and so on.

So, get rid of your negative self-talk, your doubt, and low self-esteem; you are a success! Keep up the momentum and enjoy the dining experience. Welcome to the club of Elephant Eaters. You are in good company.

Life Category Goals

Now let us establish Life Category Goals, a.k.a. Impact Goals. Recall the four Life Categories:

- Health
- Relationships
- Career
- Finances

In each category, we will establish over-arching goals that guide our actions and create performance focus. Goal setting is an important step in living with Impact. In Bite #7, you will create the Impact Action Plan in which to focus effort and strive to reach your Impact Goals.

Goals are expressions of the person you are to become. The Impact Goals bring the Impact vision into reality. The actions we take to reach our Impact Goals align with the Impact Mission-Values statement. Goals are not time based. Impact Goals are what we strive to become; they consume us. We live and breathe to achieve the Impact Goals by the Impact Mission-Values Statement standard.

The Life Category Goals (Impact Goals)

Health

> *To become healthier, to achieve greater strength, agility and balance in mind, body, spirit*

Relationships

> *To manage relationships for mutually beneficial outcomes, to better manage who is in my boat*

Career

> *To find passion and grow in my profession, to become more value-added*

Finances

> *To become a responsible steward of my finances and build wealth, to become a role model for others*

Impact Performance! Tip:

You should post these Impact Goals on your refrigerator or bathroom mirror; somewhere such that you will be reminded every day that your thoughts, conversations, behaviors, and actions should be towards achieving these goals.

Let us dive a bit deeper into the Life Categories and the Impact Goals.

Health Performance

It may be a challenge for some to become a healthier person, sound in mind, body, spirit as they may be afflicted in some manner. The idea of this goal is to become as healthy as you can be within your means and control. No matter your situation, you can improve your Health Performance and achieve balance therein.

We are not asking for miracles; we are simply stating that we desire to be more healthy and balanced in mind, body, and spirit. We can empathize with those challenged physically with limitations; however, there are people who suffer mentally and emotionally as well. Some may need professional assistance and you are encouraged to seek professional help as needed.

As we know, there are actions we can take to increase our health related performance and outcomes. It takes power and leadership to change ingrained habits, behavioral patterns, and lifestyle choices that lead to sub-optimal mental, physical and emotional performance. It takes improved Power and Self-Leadership to sustain on-going Health Performance improvement.

We will focus on the health-performance action plan in Bite #7. The point here is that we desire to become healthier in mind, body, and spirit. Greater Health Performance is critical for balance in our lives. When any aspect of our health suffers or declines in performance, it yields detrimental effects on the other Life Categories. Conversely, when we are sound in mind, body, and spirit, we are more capable of facilitating and supporting performance improvement across the other Life Categories of Relationships, Career, and Finances.

Relationship Performance

To manage relationships "for mutually-beneficial outcomes" is a worthy goal indeed. From the beginning of time, humankind has been connected via interpersonal relationships. As stated earlier, your relationships can be a great source of joy or can lead to great stress if not managed properly. A key to achieving greater strength and agility in your relationships is efficient and effective communication. It is critical to level-set expectations and to meet those expectations. Frustration occurs when a person experiences an unmet expectation, which can lead to the end of that relationship.

Consider your relationships for a moment. Is there clear and concise communication of expectations? If not, then is the other person truly at fault? Remember it takes two to tango; both parties are responsible for the success or failure to efficiently and effectively communicate and meet the other person's needs and expectations. The lack of efficient and effective two-way communication is a primary root cause of relationship issues that lead to divorce and break-ups.

It would be foolish to think this book can solve the never-ending issues associated with interpersonal relationships. The point here is that, as Elephant Eaters, we strive to manage our relationships for mutually beneficial outcomes. There are clear and concrete actions we can take to achieve this goal. It requires better control of our Power Source and better management of our Self-Leadership to deliver positive Relationship Performance and outcomes.

The Relationships Impact Performance Goal includes better management of those in your "boat." The metaphorical boat represents the people in your sphere: work, family, friends and significant others who influence your life.

"He who walks with the wise grows wise, but a companion of fools suffers harm."   Proverbs 13:20

Who Is In Your Boat?

You are the captain of your boat, the sole person responsible for setting the destination, mapping the course, preparing the boat for sail and selecting the crew to help you succeed in your voyage of life. If you have no destination, the prevailing wind of others' opinions will direct you. Therefore, it is best to have experienced and wise sailors who have traveled the rough seas of life with you at all times.

Spend time assessing your boat and its crew. Who is actually steering the boat? Who is navigating your course? Who is rowing or keeping the boat in top condition? Who is on the lookout for icebergs and sharks in the water? Are there people in your boat who are sabotaging your voyage or attempting to change your ultimate destination for their pleasure? Are there people who are along for the ride and not contributing to helping you achieve your destination (i.e. dead weight)? Who is in your boat? What role do they play?

As part of your Relationships Performance improvement effort, you will need to categorize the people in your life. Are those within your inner sphere contributing or capable of contributing to ongoing improvements in your Power Source, Self-Leadership, and Life's Outcomes or not? It is critical to your overall performance improvement and ultimate success to allow only those committed to your Impact Success in your Impact Performance! boat.

The point here is that there may be people you allow to negatively influence your thoughts, decisions, behaviors and actions (i.e. in your boat) and diminish your Power. They are not committed to your personal performance improvement. If someone is not truly committed to helping you achieve your Impact Goals, then they are not worthy of influencing you in any way. Why would you allow someone who has ulterior motives to influence your Power, much less your thoughts, decisions, conversations, or actions? A good test of whether or not someone can board your Impact boat: share your Impact Goals, Impact Vision and the Impact Performance! - Personal Performance Model (IP!-PIM), then gauge their reaction. If they laugh, smirk, or convey any sort of negative reaction, then they are not to board your Impact boat. If on the other hand, that person is supportive and positive, then they should play a role in helping you to achieve Impact Success - ships ahoy!

Boating Lessons

In your attempt to manage who is in your boat, you may need to give a few of the crew boating lessons. That is, if they are to remain within your sphere of influence, then they will need to adjust their behaviors and actions towards helping you reach your Impact Goals. Otherwise, you may have to leave them at the dock.

Do not be shy in your quest to find the right people to allow in the boat and help you improve performance. With those you desire to be in your boat, simply state, "I am improving my life. I have stated Impact Goals and I would like you to help me be successful. This is what I need from you...." Then you discuss and set expectations for future specific actions. In turn, you ask, "How can I help you to be successful? What are the specific actions I can take to help you reach your Impact goals?" In this way, you are gaining alignment, building trust and recruiting the best sailors possible to assist in your voyage (and theirs).

Walk the Plank, Eliminate Toxic Relationships

Eliminate toxic relationships from your life. Yes, you need additional Power and Self-Leadership to take the actions necessary to make someone "walk the plank" and handle properly. You may be experiencing toxicity in a relationship with a co-worker, family member, or friend. It may seem difficult or impossible to rid a toxic relationship because that person may be close to you; but you must consider whether each relationship you accept is toxic to your improvement efforts or not. We are not stating that you should isolate yourself; rather, we are suggesting for you to remove toxicity from your personal improvement efforts.

Part of your tactical performance improvement plan is to eliminate toxic relationships that cause sub-optimal performance across the Life Categories. Toxic relationships precipitate the worst in your overall performance, whereas golden relationships yield greater optimism and un-tap your improvement potential. See examples of toxic relationships in the Appendix. If you have a toxic relationship, make them walk the plank.

Eliminate the bad, and accentuate the good relationships in your life.

To improve all aspects of our lives we need positive and productive relationships. We need those who are committed to our success and who help facilitate our Impact Action Plan in our boat. As you can imagine, some of those in our lives are elephants. An elephant can throw us off-course, slow us down, poke a hole in our boat and even sink our boat. You will need additional Power Source and Self-Leadership performance to bring the right sailors, first mates, and navigators into your boat to overcome the rough seas of life.

Remember your Relationships Performance Goal is to strive for mutually beneficial outcomes and to manage who is in your boat more effectively.

Career Performance

To find passion in your profession is an honorable and admirable goal. To become more value-added is a basic tenet of Impact Performance! What does it mean to find passion in your profession? In general, you find excitement and a degree of autonomy, mastery, and purpose in your work. If you are a nurse and enjoy helping others to overcome their ailments, you likely possess passion for your work. However, some of us may view our work as menial and not enjoyable. You may be searching for another position all together. No matter the situation, it is important to find passion in your work. As the saying goes, "If you enjoy what you do, you won't work another day in your life."

The key here is to seek and focus on the aspects of your work that excite you and make your work more enjoyable. You spend most of your waking hours working, so why not seek more pleasure from the experience? Perhaps you can find passion in helping your company sell more products and / or services, improve current products, reduce customer complaints, start a recycle program, become more sustainable, initiate a wellness program, etc. It may take significant Power Source and Self-Leadership Performance to adjust your general attitude towards work; this is understandable. To increase your Career performance, seek passion for what you do.

For those who do not work or who possess a very high work misery index, then focus on your passions in life, such as a hobby. If you cannot find passion in your current work, are not presently in the workforce, or are retired, then the idea is to spend quality time pursuing the things you enjoy that are productive. For example, there are many who enjoy gardening, music, charity work, etc. In this case, your Impact Career Goal is to find passion in your hobbies. Some people start new businesses from their hobbies to create multiple streams of income.

To become more value added simply means that the benefits of your employment far out-weigh your employer's cost to employ you. The more value you provide to your employer and your profession, the more pride and recognition you will realize. If you are outside of the workforce, then the same applies to your hobbies. Your hobbies should be value-added; that is, the benefits of your activities should far out-weigh the costs.

To seek more challenge in your profession affords the opportunity for growth. If it is too easy, how are you growing? To become a master of your profession, seek the greatest challenges and overcome those challenges; learn from the experience and you will become more valuable. You may seek additional training, attend night school, or simply ask for more responsibility. In any case, you are to seek more challenge in your work to improve your Career Challenge Performance.

One definition of work performance:

Productivity = Aptitude + Attitude + Organizational Support

In your desire to improve Career Performance, keep this equation in mind. You can take more control and deliver more productivity (a.k.a. "presenteeism") by achieving greater Aptitude through accepting more challenge (i.e. learning) and by achieving greater Attitude through seeking more passion for your work. You should ask for more organizational support as needed to become more productive in general. The suggestion here is to make sure that you have done your homework before asking for more support such that your employer sees the return on the investment.

Recall that most of us associate who we are to what we do professionally. As your Career Performance increases, your sense of self-actualization will increase; self-worth and self-esteem will grow too.

Finances Performance

To become a responsible steward of your finances and to build wealth not only comprises the Impact Finances Goal, but these are basic tenets of Impact Performance! The idea here is not of greed. Our goal here is to change the habits and impulses that lead us into debt and to use our funds for the greater good (i.e. creating jobs and giving to charity).

The savings rate in the U.S. is near an all-time low, and foreclosures and bankruptcies at an all-time high. If you have fallen on hard times, that is a crushing blow and it will take time in which to recover; we empathize with your situation. No matter your personal situation, you can and should become a better steward of your finances. We will discuss the finances performance action plan in Bite #7.

For now, it is important to realize the need to better manage finances and build wealth for your family. To this point, we are referring to your responsibility to become a role model for others and especially to your children in terms of money management. It may take significant improvement in your Power Source and Self-Leadership to effect change in your Finances Life Category. No matter the circumstance, your money management performance can be improved. You will identify the financial elephants in Bite #6.

As we all know (but do not necessarily practice), there are tools and principles of money management, which help to create wealth. In the context of Finances Performance, we are referring to net worth given by the following equation:

Net Worth = Assets − Liabilities.

Finances Performance refers specifically to your ability to increase assets and decrease liabilities to generate greater net worth (i.e. wealth). Your Finances Performance efforts are to create more net worth for you and your family.

As mentioned earlier, financial matters are a root cause of divorce. The goal of being a responsible financial steward and building wealth is a shared goal for married and committed couples (an important element of Couplism). It is vital for couples to share common disciplined actions regarding their finances. Since money management, rather the lack thereof, is a causal effect to marital distress, couples should be completely committed to the Impact Finances Goal, Impact Objective, milestones, and action plan to improve Finances Performance.

The ability to better manage and increase revenue, reduce spending and invest more wisely yields greater Finances Performance. Ultimately, Elephant Eaters strive to become financial role models through their demonstrated Finances Performance improvement and in helping others financially (i.e. their families and charities).

Balance Across the Life Categories

Elephant Eaters strive for balance across their Life's Categories. Balance is a determinate of Impact Success. It is vital to strive for balance. Reread this section as needed; it is important.

Health Performance, Relationships Performance, Career Performance, and Finances Performance are equally important and interconnected. One is not more or less important than another is important. A key point is not to become one-dimensional. If you focus too much on one Life

Category, the others suffer improvement opportunity loss. A performance focus with measurable improvement across all Life Categories will yield greater performance in each category vs. a myopic singular focus on one. When you are down in one Life Category, never cease to seek improvement across all of your Life Categories.

Imagine a stool where the legs of the stool are the Life Categories. Each is essential in keeping you up and balanced. Now if you are lacking or falter along one of the legs of the stool, the stool becomes unbalanced. Most of your energy tends to focus on that leg. There would be urgency and priority to drive action, of course. This is understandable and encouraged. However, keep in mind that improvement in the other Life Categories will help to prop-up the leg that needs immediate attention as all are connected.

When you are unbalanced, the tendency is to hang-on and survive the storm. Again, this is understandable. Always strive for balance and improvement in each of the Life Categories. A performance focus and striving for balance will help you to avoid the dreaded "downward spiral." We have all seen someone get down in one area of their life, e.g. a relationship "gone bad," and the next thing you know other aspects of their life falter. Elephants Eaters know and understand this potential pothole in the road of life and avoid it with balance!

Improvement and increasing strength in the legs of the stool provide a basis for acceleration in life. How can you "blast-off" from an unbalanced platform?

Elephant Eaters strive for balance across the Life Categories Period! Remember, balance is a determinate of Impact Success. All of the Life Categories are interconnected. This means that the performance level in one affects the others.

If performance improves in a given Life Category, it will help to improve the performance of the other Life Categories.

If your Health performance suffers, it will have a negative effect on your Career performance, which will have a negative effect on your Finances, and Relationships performance as well. If your Relationships Performance is on a downward trend, then it will bring down your Career Performance, which will hurt your Finances Performance, and so on. Conversely, if your Relationships performance is progressing forward, that improvement will have a positive impact on your Health performance, which will have a positive impact on your Finances and Career Life Categories. Improvement in the Career Life Category will afford improvement in Finances and Relationships Categories, and so on. It is paramount to strive for improvement and to eat the elephants in each of the Life Categories as improvement in any category helps you to achieve improvement in the other categories.

Of note, stress can quadruple your likelihood of Alzheimer's disease. There is a clear connection between physical, mental and emotional habits and overall health status. Remember, balance relieves stress and affords acceleration.

Again, the Life Categories are interconnected; you should not sacrifice performance focus in one category over another. Self-Leadership is the glue that holds the Life Categories together. The greater your self-awareness of the interconnectivity of the Life Categories, then the greater is your ability to balance - hence greater overall Impact Performance! Your thoughts, decisions, behaviors, and actions in one Life Category will have causal effect on the other Life Categories. As such, it is important to adopt a performance focus and strive to achieve the Impact Goals simultaneously across all Life Categories.

Improved Self-Leadership affords improved balance.

We have all seen people who are one-dimensional. That is, they may be so career focused they suffer health problems. Perhaps you know someone so focused on money they cannot maintain a healthy relationship. Some focus purely on the body but neglect the mental and emotional aspects of their health. We have seen the detrimental effects of poor money management on a person's health, relationships, and their career. Perhaps some of us perform very well in work relationships but perform poorly with non-work related relationship performance?

Elephant Eaters strive to become balanced which elevates the development of strength and agility in all sub-categories of the Life Categories. Elephant Eaters need this balance of strength and agility across the Life Categories to overcome all impediments in reaching their Impact Goals and to increase the probability of Impact Success.

Below is a summary of the Impact Goals. You should be able to memorize these easily. Self-Leadership, fueled by additional Power, is to be directed towards achieving these goals and striving for balance across each.

Life Category Goals Summary

> *To become healthier, to achieve greater strength, agility and balance in mind, body, spirit*

> *To manage my relationships for mutually beneficial outcomes, to better manage who is in my boat*

To find passion and challenge in my profession, to become more value-added

To become a responsible steward of my finances and build wealth, to become a role model for others

Ok, let us review. Thus far, you have devoured the first four Bites of the elephant by:

1. Embracing the Impact Mission-Values Statement
2. Envisioning Yourself as an Impact Person
3. Benchmarking Your Life Categories' Performance Levels
4. Redefining Success and Setting Goals in the Four Life Categories

Additionally you have benchmarked your Power Source and Self-Leadership and gained further understanding of the need for balance across the Life Categories.

You are gaining momentum. You have clearly defined who you are and who you desire to be. It should be clear as well that you are a redefined success. You have clearly established goals for your life, which means, you are poised for Impact Performance! Great job!

In the following Bites, we will establish clear performance measures and time-based objectives of your performance efforts as well as the action plan to achieve.

Are you still hungry?

Bite #5: Establish Your Impact Performance! Measurement System

"Measure what is measureable, and make measureable what is not so."

Galileo

Unless you accurately monitor and track performance, how can you demonstrate performance improvement? How do you know if you are going up or down in personal performance?

Too often, we focus on the wrong measure, which leads to misguided effort and poor overall results; and yet, we may celebrate success, but in error. The selection of improper measures typically leads to an erosion of overall performance.

For example, too often, people will use a weigh scale to measure their body weight, which is fine, but they conclude they need to lose weight. Why? Is it to look better and to become more accepted by societal norms? This is misguided thinking. Crash diets and diet pills are exceedingly unhealthy and dangerous. A more appropriate measure is percent body fat. If a person desires to become healthier in terms of body performance, percent body fat targets are appropriate (consult your doctor). The tactics used to lose weight are invariably unhealthy and reduce overall Health Performance (not only physical, but mental, and emotional too). Interestingly, a person focused on percent body fat (appropriate for their age and height) via a healthy lifestyle will likely lose weight and not suffer the ill effects of "lose weight fast" swindles. Weight loss is typically unsustainable without lifestyle changes (and usually leads to further mental and emotional stress). The point here is to choose wisely when establishing specific performance measures.

The Impact definition of "performance" is the measure of a resultant outcome over time or other comparable basis. In this context you are to establish a measurement system to provide accurate feedback regarding your progress over time. Note you have established the benchmarked performance levels in Bite #3, which constitute the basis of performance comparison.

The most salient question is how to measure and demonstrate Impact Performance! improvement across the Self-System: the Power Source (input), Self-Leadership (process), and in the Life Categories (output).

There are three methods to measure Impact Performance! These are:

1. Journaling
2. Accountability Partner feedback, and
3. Mentoring

Journaling

Daily journaling is the most important measure of your personal performance improvement effort. We are not referring to a dairy; rather, we are arguing for a personal commitment to log your daily improvement efforts across the Life Categories: Health, Relationships, Career and Finances.

Journaling puts a finger on the pulse of your performance improvement efforts from a personal perspective. The Impact Performance! Journal is broken down into journal entries for each of the four Life Categories daily, as well as the Power Source and Self-Leadership weekly. The Impact Journal is available on-line at www.ip-getmoving.com.

A powerful aspect of journaling is the ability to look back and see how far you have progressed. Retrospection can be very telling and motivating. You capture your feelings and actions in the moment; then you begin to see clearly how you face challenges in your life over time. If you have never made journal entries before, it takes some practice. The ability to chronicle your progress becomes invaluable with time as you see the positive change and positive outcomes unfold; it is a written expression of your success story.

Following is an example of an Impact Performance! daily journal entry. Here you notice that you are to input your current performance level (CPL) and your stated milestone in each of the Life Categories. In this way, you see your near-term target performance levels daily. This daily reminder affords reinforcement of your performance focus and helps you stay focused. This daily reminder is vital in improving your Self-Leadership (i.e. improvement of thought patterns, decisions, behaviors and actions).

The journal entry for each Life Category should reflect your daily actions to improve in the sub-categories of that respective Life Category. For example, regarding Health Performance, you should journal any activities pertinent to your efforts to improve physically, mentally and emotionally during that day. You may not have the opportunity to improve in each of the sub-categories of a given Life Category on that specific day. However, the intention is that you will focus on the sub-categories of the Life Categories daily and note actions taken in your journal.

What actions have you taken today to improve in each of the twelve sub-categories of Impact Performance!?

A key to unlocking your performance potential and to eat the elephant is a daily focus on that which is most important in your life; i.e. the Life Categories. When you begin to journal about your focused improvement efforts, it becomes infectious. You will desire more and more improvement when you note and observe your personal commitment and positive results. Often the mere act of journaling leads to personal performance improvement.

As you witness and chronicle your personal improvement, you become more self-aware and develop more self-control. In effect, you are enabling Self-Leadership and gaining more Power with self-reflection. Your improvement directed efforts leap off the pages of your journal. It is a record of your achievements. You reveal the thought patterns, decisions, behaviors and actions you exhibit daily towards reaching your stated Impact Performance! Milestones. We will discuss objectives and milestones in detail in the next Bite. Your energy, desire, will to succeed, motivation and courage to stand-up, confront and eat the elephant are displayed and chronicled...it is a microscope into the new "Impact you." Your journal captures positive change and personal growth, for you document your process of on-going Impact Success. Thus, journaling affords the ability to take proper control of your actions for on-going personal improvement.

Once you master the art of journaling and taking action-control for on-going improvement, you are positioning yourself well to help others succeed. You have a record of your success story to share with others. Honest journaling takes Power. You may be living in denial and not facing the truth about your performance. Now is the time to chronicle your performance-focused actions, monitor your performance, and move forward to reach each of your Life Category milestones.

How to Journal, Daily

On the next page is an example of a daily journal entry. Here are the steps to journaling daily:

1. Enter your current performance level (CPL) for the Health Performance Life Category. You *feel* this performance level that day.
2. Enter your stated milestone; this is your target.
3. Next, you are to journal your actions towards reaching the stated milestone in the Health Performance Life Category. What did you do that day to improve in the sub-categories of the Health Performance Life Category (physical, mental, emotional)? Write it down; this is tangible proof.
4. Move to the next Life Category, Relationship Performance and so on.

Importantly and interestingly, your CPL entries will likely vary from day to day. This is natural. Expect variation in daily performance. Note however, you should expect improvement with time as you journal your performance focused actions. You will begin to experience improvement in each of the Life Categories with a performance focus and striving for balance across each.

In this example, you see entries for each category. Even though this person is lower in their Health Performance vs. the other categories, there is a performance focus in each Life Category - i.e. balance.

Example of a daily Impact Performance! journal entry:

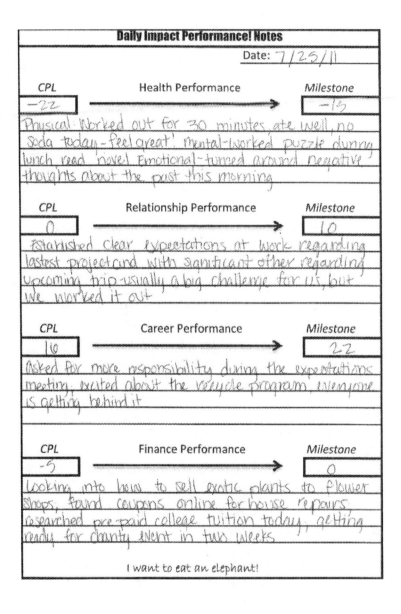

Daily Impact Performance! Notes

Date: 7/25/11

CPL   Health Performance   Milestone

-22   -13

Physical: Worked out for 30 minutes, ate well, no soda today - feel great! Mental-worked puzzle during lunch, read novel. Emotional-turned around negative thoughts about the past this morning

CPL   Relationship Performance   Milestone

0   10

Established clear expectations at work regarding lastest project and with significant other regarding upcoming trip usually a big challenge for us, but we worked it out

CPL   Career Performance   Milestone

10   22

Asked for more responsibility during the expectations meeting, excited about the recycle program, everyone is getting behind it

CPL   Finance Performance   Milestone

-5   0

Looking into how to sell exotic plants to flower shops, found coupons online for house repairs, researched pre-paid college tuition today, getting ready for charity event in two weeks

I want to eat an elephant!

Accountability Partner

The responsibility of the Accountability Partner is to hold you accountable for your improvement efforts and Impact Success. Therefore, you should seek someone who has the moxie to call you out and give you honest feedback. Your Accountability Partner should be your spouse / significant other if you are married or in a committed relationship. If you are not in a committed relationship or married, then select someone trustworthy to fill this role. Keep in mind; you may be an Accountability Partner for someone one day.

The Accountability Partner is to help you adopt a performance focus on your Power Source, Self-Leadership and the Life Categories. Additionally, they hold you accountable for striving for balance.

Specifically, Accountability Partners are to encourage the ability to:

- Draw upon your Power Source to persevere,
- Manage Self-Leadership with a performance focus,
- Progress towards your Impact Goals,
- Live the Impact Mission-Values statement, and, of course,
- Eat the elephant!

If you are not making progress, "hit a wall," or become stymied, they are to offer encouragement, inspire you, and motivate you. They are to remind you of how far you have come and how far you can go. They help facilitate a life of Impact Performance! Remember, you are not alone in this endeavor of eating the elephant.

You are to meet with your Accountability Partner weekly and discuss the components of your Power Source (energy, desire, intrinsic motivation, courage) and Self-Leadership (thought patterns, decisions, behaviors, actions). Importantly, talk about your elephants. Discuss the people, places, things (patterns), and circumstances that hold you back. Often, the consistency of shining a light on the elephants will yield the utensils needed to eat them!

How to Journal, Weekly

You are to enter the feedback from your Accountability Partner weekly meeting. Remember they are the mirror that reflects your Impact Performance!

1. Enter your current performance level (CPL) for your Power Source. You *feel* this performance level when meeting with your Accountability Partner.
2. Enter your stated milestone; this is your target.
3. Next, you are to journal your actions towards reaching the stated milestone in your Power Source. What did you do that that week to improve in the components of the Power Source? How have you performed that week in terms of your energy, desire, motivation, and courage to eat the elephant? Your Accountability Partner is to provide direct, honest, and actionable feedback. Write it down.
4. Next, address your Self-Leadership performance. Enter your CPL and your milestone.
5. Enter the feedback from your Accountability Partner. Have they witnessed any positive or negative changes in your thoughts, decisions, behaviors or actions across the Life Categories? What is the feedback regarding your ability to balance across the Life Categories? Write it down.

6. Discuss your #1 elephants. What are the biggest, meanest, ugliest elephants standing in your path of improvement? Are you more capable of eating them? Write it down.

Note your CPL entries will likely vary week to week. This is natural. Expect some minor variation in weekly Power Source and Self-Leadership performance (typically much less than the observed variation of daily Life Category Performance).

In the example given, this person has a perceived negative performance level in both their Power Source and Self-Leadership. Are they a failure? No, of course they are not. Is there urgency to get moving? Yes.

In addition, we see this person is capturing the weekly discussion points from their meeting. This keen performance focus on the Power Source and Self-Leadership affords a high probability of Impact Success.

Example of a weekly Accountability Partner Impact Performance! journal entry:

Weekly Accountability Partner Review

Date: 7/30/11

Enter the weekly feedback from your Account Partner below:

CPL	Power Source	Milestone
-30	→	-20

My AP sees that I have more energy these days and that I'm not full of excuses anymore. Now that I'm improving my motivation and desire to eat the elephant are greater than ever. He says I'm more confident - it was very encouraging. We talked about how to maintain courage in the face of challenge.

CPL	Self-Leadership	Milestone
-12	→	0

He reminded me of the importance to improve my thought patterns which lead to positive action and outcomes. We've now seeing my spending habits improve and my credit card debt going down! My health has improved too. I am now more focused on decisions and behaviors in all my relationships (especially at work).

www.ip-getmoving.com

Calculation of Your Monthly Impact Performance!

At the end of each month, you are to:

1. Go to the monthly tracking section of your IP! journal.

2. On the first page of the Monthly Impact Performance! Tracking log, enter your CPL in each sub-category for the current and previous month and note the change from the previous month.

3. On the second page, enter the average of the performance across the sub-categories of each Life Category from the first page (for example, take the average of physical, mental and emotion and enter for the Health Performance Life Category); enter your milestones.

4. Last, take the average of all the sub-categories to calculate your overall monthly Impact Performance! Note, mathematically it is not technically correct to simply average across the Life Categories. You need to average across all twelve of the sub-categories to yield a more accurate value for your Impact Performance!

5. Enter your Impact Performance! in the table. You will have to enter the values from the previous months to note your positive performance trend.

Evaluate. Interpret.

Do you see any change in sub-category performance from the previous month? Are there negative differences (going down), positive differences (going up), or a mixture of both? A negative dip in sub-category performance indicates immediate action and focus. Remember, however, not to let up in any of the other sub-categories; always strive for balance. Conversely, if you note improvement from the previous month in a given sub-category, then celebrate with your Accountability Partner; he or she helped you earn it.

An interesting point in this self-analysis is the average monthly Life Category Performance based on your sub-category values compared to your daily journal entries. When you average the sub-categories and calculate the monthly Health Performance Life Category level, is the value close to the daily entries made for Health Performance towards the end of the month? This affords a calibration of how well you are assessing daily performance in the Life Categories. If the average of the monthly sub-category numbers does not match the daily Life Category performance levels (towards the end of the month) and are off by > 5, then you should focus more on your daily performance in each of the Life Category sub-categories. Keep in the top of your mind, Life Category performance is a function of the performance of the sub-categories. Now, if the numbers tend to match, then your internal calibration of the sub-category measurement mechanism is adequate.

Regarding your monthly average Life Category performance, have you reached any milestones along the Impact Performance! Continuum? If so, then celebrate; reinforce your positive momentum. Sustainable positive change is a function of reaching new heights of personal performance, enjoying the view from the new vantage point...then seeking even greater heights.

Most importantly, is your overall monthly Impact Performance! trending upward, more positive? If not, then spend more time with other Elephant Eaters and your Accountability Partner for their support. Your elephants are holding you back; never forget they are ever-present. In each of the Life Categories, you have an elephant staring you down and blocking your path of personal improvement. If you feel as though you have plateaued in performance, then seek additional help and guidance from Elephant Hunters; they are passionate about helping others eat the elephant.

In the example given, we see positive improvement in each sub-category (first page). No milestones had been reached, but this person is close to celebrating the Finances Performance milestone (second page). Note their Finances milestone is "0". They simply desire to be average compared to everyone else (per the Performance Continuum), but since they are making improvement progress, in the safari, they are a success! Also note she is demonstrating overall Impact Performance! improvement (within 5 months they improved from -30 to -4). This is an example of a true elephant eater.

Example of the first page of the Monthly Impact Performance! Tracking log:

Monthly Impact Performance! Tracking

Date: 7/30/11

Enter your current performance level (CPL) for each Life Category sub-category and note the change from the previous month.

Health Sub-category Performance   Change +/-

Body Physical	-40	5
Mind - Mental	-6	9
Spirit - Emotional	-20	5

Relationship Sub-category Performance

Work	0	6
Family	5	11
Friends	5	10
Significant Other	-10	10

Career Sub-category Performance

Passion	10	0
Challenge	22	7

Finances Sub-category Performance

Income	0	5
Spending	-20	5
Investing	5	10

I want to eat an elephant!

Example of the second page of the Monthly Impact Performance! Tracking log:

Monthly Impact Performance! Tracking		

Date: 7/30/11

Calculate the average performance in each Life Category.

Average the current performance levels across the sub-categories of each Life Category and list below:

Life Category Performance		Milestones
Health Performance...	-22	-15
Relationship Performance...	0	10
Career Performance...	16	22
Finances Performance...	-5	0

Celebrate any Milestones achieved this month. You've earned it.

Calculate Overall Impact Performance!

Average the current performance levels across all 12 sub-categories and enter your overall Impact Performance! below:

Impact Performance!			
January		July	-4
February		August	
March	-30	September	
April	-22	October	
May	-20	November	
June	-11	December	

www.ip-getmoving.com

117

You may think that daily journaling and a weekly Accountability Partner meeting is a lot of work, but you should remember what is at stake - living a life of Impact Performance! and the ability to help others succeed. In addition, once you get on a roll with journaling and a weekly discussion with your Accountability Partner, it becomes a priority and routine. It will become a natural way of living. The act of measurement tracking and review will bolster a keen performance focus. Measurement is the heart of Impact Performance! When it beats, you excel.

Please remember that negative values for any sub-category do not constitute failure in any sense. The Impact Performance! Continuum is a relative scale. If you are performing in the negative range for any sub-category, it simply means that you need to get moving!

Mentoring

Another component of your performance measurement is your Mentor(s). The role of the Mentor is simple. This is someone who has demonstrated mastery of a given Life Category. It is likely you will have more than one Mentor as very few have mastered all of Life's Categories. If needed, seek a Mentor in each of the four Life Categories.

The Mentor is someone who has overcome obstacles in the respective Life Category and can help you navigate from your current position towards your desired Impact Goal. For example, as part of the Health Performance Life Category, you should find a Mentor who is skilled in the areas of mind, body and spirit, not just the body alone. In the Relationships Life Category, find someone who is skilled in communication and the ability to level-set expectations across the sub-categories. With regard to the Career Life Category, you should find a Mentor who knows how to find passion and to add value to the work environment and / or hobbies to be more productive. They can help you to create more challenge in your career to promote professional growth. Regarding the Finances Life Category, you should be very selective here and find someone who you can trust regarding matters of income generation, spending habits and investing - not just investing alone.

The characteristic of the Mentor is someone who can truly help you reach the next level of performance in the respective Life Category. Note you may need to find another Mentor once you have reached the next level of performance (e.g. a given milestone); find someone who can help you perform at the next level. Again, the role of the Mentor is someone who can help shine a light on the path to greater performance; to improve, you need guidance and to "walk with the wise."

View your Mentor as a coach and navigator of your boat. They are committed to your success. You should consult with your mentor as needed; there is not a set period or written requirement here other than your daily journal entry of the advice given and indicated actions.

Recall that one of the main impediments of Impact Success is a lack of an accurate measurement system. The combination of your journal entries, accountability partner feedback and your mentor's advice will paint a clear picture of personal performance improvement progress and actions needed to stay on-track. They are to help you identify elephants on an on-going basis as well.

To summarize, your general measurement system is comprised of journaling, accountability partnership and mentorship. These three components of measurement will reflect your progress. Your feelings are justified if this seems out-of-the-box and uncomfortable. This feeling is one of positive change and a new way of thinking, behaving and living. The people you choose to be part of your success venture in eating elephants are critical; choose them wisely.

At this point, obtain a journal and begin journaling. Also, select and solicit the help of your Accountability Partner and your Mentor(s). Share with them the IP!-PIM and the fact they are now in your boat to play a pivotal role in your progress towards a life of Impact Performance! They should be passionate about your improvement success.

Take a deep breath for a quick review. Thus far, you have accomplished much in your personal improvement journey. Your performance improvement so far includes:

1. Embracing the Impact Mission-Values Statement
2. Envisioning Yourself as an Impact Person
3. Benchmarking Your Life Categories' Performance Levels
4. Redefining Success and Setting Life Categories Goals (Impact Goals)
5. Establishing Your Measurement System

Now it is time to identify the people, places, things, and circumstances that hold you back and stymie your improvement efforts. Let us identify your elephants, so you can eat them.

Bite #6: Identify Your Elephants

"Determine the thing that can and shall be done, and then we shall find the way."

Abraham Lincoln

How can you eat the elephants if you do not identify them? Most of us live in denial of the need to improve and yet the elephant remains. We acquiesce to the existence of outside and inside forces that hold us back. Our very existence is defined by limitations and our ability / inability to push those limits outward. To grow, prosper, and progress, that is, to improve our performance, we must first identify those forces that keep us from reaching our stated Impact Goals, and then overcome those negative forces (i.e. elephants).

In this Bite, you are to identify the elephants that are in the way of achieving your Life Category Goals. Recall that each Life Category is broken-down into sub-categories. As such, you are to identify the elephants that hold you back in each of the sub-categories.

The Impact ForceLine helps identify your elephants. The ForceLine is a visual illustration of the positive forces that push you forward toward your goal and the negative forces aligned against you. The aim here is to clearly state with conviction that which stands in your way of performance improvement.

Identify Your Elephants

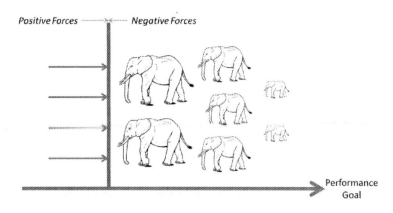

Positive Forces ···········>·<··········· Negative Forces

Performance
Goal

You are to identify those elephants, so that they can indeed be eaten, never to return. As needed, draw a vertical line and a horizontal line as shown above. List the positive forces helping you succeed and the negative forces holding you back. What are the elephants keeping your from achieving your performance goals?

There are all types of elephants of every size and shape (some obvious and some not so obvious). It may seem as though you have unique elephants staring you down. Even though you may feel as though your elephants align uniquely against you, keep in mind that since the beginning of human existence, there have been challenges and the desire to overcome those challenges; so it is likely others have faced similar challenges. You are not alone in the hunt.

Now you are to list your elephants in each of the Life Category sub-categories.

Think in terms of your Life Category / Impact Goals. What is holding you back or standing in your way? What is stopping you from achieving your stated Impact Goals?

Life Category Goals Summary

> *To become healthier, to achieve greater strength, agility and balance in mind, body, spirit*

> *To manage my relationships for mutually beneficial outcomes, to better manage who is in my boat*

> *To find passion and grow in my profession, to become more value-added*

> *To become a responsible steward of my finances and build wealth, to become a role model for others*

Now recall that you established benchmarked performance in the twelve sub-categories of the Life Categories. What is keeping you from progressing forward to a higher level of performance in each sub-category? What are the negative forces that are against you?

Write down the primary elephants in each sub-category. Try to put as much definition and dimension as possible when detailing your elephants. This is important in regards to establishing your Impact Action Plan to eat the elephant. The better identified, the easier to eat.

You should spend ample time on this exercise; do not rush through the identification of your elephants. In addition, you need to be completely honest with yourself. You will not do yourself any favors by listing easy to overcome elephants. List the biggest, ugliest, meanest elephants staring you down.

If you can overcome and eat the biggest impediments to performance improvement progress, then the smaller ones will be easier to digest. In addition, if you believe a person is an elephant, then list them. We will discuss the "eat the elephant" action plan in the next Bite. Do not worry about hurting someone's feelings; you are simply making an honest list of elephants at this point. This will likely be an illuminating exercise.

Keep in mind that your lack of Power and Self-Leadership (e.g. negative thought and behavioral patterns) may be elephants. Negative attitudes and negative self-perception are elephants as well.

Let us hunt.

Health Performance Elephants

List the elephants that hold you back from higher levels of Health Performance in these sub-categories:

Body – Physical

_____

_____

_____

Mind – Mental

_____

_____

_____

Spirit - Emotional

_____

_____

_____

Relationships Performance Elephants

List the elephants that hold you back from higher levels of Relationships Performance in these sub-categories:

Work

_____
_____
_____

Family

_____
_____
_____

Friends

_____
_____
_____

Significant Other

_____
_____
_____

Career Performance Elephants

List the elephants that hold you back from higher levels of Career Performance in these sub-categories:

Passion

_____
_____
_____

Challenge

_____

_____

_____

Finances Performance Elephants

List the elephants that hold you back from higher levels of Finances Performance in these sub-categories:

Income

_____

_____

_____

Spending

_____

_____

_____

Investing

_____

_____

_____

Now go back over the list carefully. Are there any persons, places, things, circumstances that overlap as elephants in more than one sub-category? Is there an elephant that appears in more than one sub-category? If so, then this may create some urgency in your action planning in the next Bite.

If you listed at least one elephant in each of the twelve sub-categories of performance, then you have at least twelve elephants listed. That seems like a large herd of intimidating elephants. However, you should peruse this list with confidence as you have now identified that which holds you back from achieving personal performance improvement success. You are close to confronting each one.

Recall, your foundation for eating the elephant is the Impact Mission-Values statement. Your Self-Leadership growth is based upon living the Impact Mission-Values statement. This is your foundation for eating the identified elephants. You will need to summon greater Power to initiate positive change and to confront the elephants head-on. Identify with the elements of the Power Source; envision the Power to initiate positive change.

Let us recap: you have made huge progress; this is where you stand at this moment. Your on-going Impact Success includes:

1. Embracing the Impact Mission-Values Statement
2. Envisioning Yourself as an Impact Person
3. Benchmarking Your Life Categories' Performance Levels
4. Redefining Success and Setting Life Categories Goals
5. Establishing Your Measurement System
6. Identifying the Elephants

Up to this point you have been preparing for action. Your plan to move forward and eat the elephant is discussed in Bite #7. There is nothing standing in your way of improvement, not even an elephant. Think positive to be positive.

Bite #7: Create the "Eat the Elephant" Impact Action Plan

"An idea is just an idea until it is put into action."

Now that you have identified the specific elephants that stand in your way in each of the Life Categories, you have a decision to make. Either you can continue to acquiesce to the existence of each one, or you can eat the elephant. If you commit to eating the elephant, then you commit to overcoming that which limits your vision, your ability to expand your world, and your future. Committed? Great! Move forward!

In Bite #6, Identify Your Elephants, you listed your elephants in each sub-category of the Life Categories. Your initial Impact Action Plan is to focus on the top elephants in each Life Category. Some may argue that you should start with the smaller, more easily digested elephants, but that is errant thinking. Your initial effort is to eat the biggest, meanest, ugliest, and most fearsome elephant in each Life Category first. Then you can eat the second most intimidating elephant in each category, and then the third, etc. Those will be much easier to eat.

You will experience that once you have conquered your greatest fear and overcome your greatest challenge in each Life Category, truly anything is possible.

Now go back and pick the most intimidating elephants in each of the Life Categories and list here:

Initial Impact Action Plan Elephant List

#1 Health Performance Elephant

_____

#1 Relationships Performance Elephant

_____

#1 Career Performance Elephant

_____

#1 Finances Performance Elephant

_____

Now, establish your time-based objectives for eliminating the barriers to personal improvement; i.e. the deadline to eat the #1 elephants. This is your line in the sand; stick to it.

Impact Objectives

Your Impact Objectives are to eliminate the #1 identified elephants in the Life Categories in a given timeframe. In your enthusiasm to improve your life, you may develop other time-based objectives; however, the focus here is to set a timetable for the elimination of your #1 elephants in each Life Category.

As such, select a date in the future such that those elephants will no longer stand in your way. You have stated Impact Goals; now is the time to decide when you will eliminate the greatest negative force holding you back.

In each Life Category, write down the date you expect to eat the elephant.

Eat the Health Performance Elephant by date: _____

Eat the Relationships Elephant by date: _____

Eat the Career Elephant by date: _____

Eat the Finances Elephant by date: _____

You should be somewhat aggressive in your timing. Otherwise, you may not achieve significant progress. Often, the timetable is too far into the future. As such, other priorities and old patterns emerge which derail your efforts and you lose performance focus.

Make a commitment regarding your timing to eat the elephant. Again, no one said it would be easy, but without a given timeframe and a line in the sand, it will not happen. Otherwise, you would have eaten the elephant already.

Milestones

Milestones are target levels of performance in each of the four Life Categories on the Impact Performance! Continuum. You are to establish time-based milestones to mark progress in each of the Life Categories. As you proceed to eat the elephant, your performance will improve. Recall the benchmarking in Bite #3. List the average performance level in each of the Life Categories now:

Benchmarked Health Performance: _____

Benchmarked Relationships Performance: _____

Benchmarked Career Performance: _____

Benchmarked Finances Performance: _____

Now establish milestones in each category. Write down the performance level you aim to achieve in a given timeframe. These dates do not necessarily correspond to the Impact Objective dates (i.e. when you have eaten the #1 elephants). In fact, the milestones should be much shorter timeframes. The aim here is to denote progress in the effort to eat the elephant along the Impact Performance! Continuum. For example, you may indicate that your #1 Career Elephant is the lack of academic training. You are going back to school to obtain a specific degree that may take two years to complete and eat the Career Elephant. A milestone would be to register for the first class or to take the entrance exam (e.g. the GMAT for an MBA program) by a given date in the near future.

The initial milestones give you something to shoot for in the near-term; they will help you to stay on-track and maintain a performance focus. When seeking to achieve Impact Performance!, you need early wins to gain and maintain momentum. Achievement of the milestones provides near-term focus and the ability to celebrate early in your improvement endeavor.

For example, you may have a benchmarked Finances Performance level of -30; your initial milestone may be to achieve a -25 in the next two months (a positive shift of 5 points). This will take concerted effort to demonstrate this significant achievement to yourself and your Accountability Partner. Recall that you have shared the benchmarked performance levels with your Accountability Partner and they are to facilitate progress. In addition, you are to make journal entries to note your daily progress towards the milestones in each Life Category (remember this helps to provide daily focus on what is truly important). You cannot make a 5-point improvement along a Life Category

Performance Continuum in two months without tangible evidence that you are making progress towards eating that respective Life Category elephant and improving in the respective sub-categories.

Enter the target Impact Performance! milestone in each Life Category with the target date below:

Initial Life Category Milestones

Health Performance: _____ Date: _____

Relationships Performance: _____ Date: _____

Career Performance: _____ Date: _____

Finances Performance: _____ Date: _____

Wow, you are truly making progress now. In this Bite alone, you have chosen a date to eat the #1 elephant in each Life Category and established near-term milestones along the Performance Continuum in each Life Category. Now, post the Eat the Elephant dates and the milestones alongside your Impact Goals such that you can see them each day and remind yourself daily of your performance focus.

Strategies and Tactics to Eat the Elephant

This is the "how to" part of your action plan to eat the elephant.

Every day is a gift. Every day you wake is an opportunity to enrich your life and the lives of others. As of this moment, this day, which thoughts will occupy your mind, what decisions will you make, what will be your conversations, what behaviors will you exhibit, and what actions will you take to improve your life and the lives of others? Will you live a life of Impact Performance!?

To eat the elephant and sustain performance improvement, your strategies are to:

- Live the Impact Mission-Values Statement daily
- Fuel Self-Leadership with more Power Source
- Exert Greater Management of Self-Leadership
- Measure Performance and Take Action-Control
- Employ Elephant Eater Tactics, and
- Strive for Balance.

At this point, you have identified the elephants and established a measurement system to see your improvement. Now is the time to put forth effort to realize tangible improvement results.

The foundation for action is the Impact Mission-Values statement; now is the time to live it.

Let us review that for which you stand. These attributes should dictate your thoughts, decision-making paradigm, behaviors and actions.

Live the Impact Mission-Values Statement Daily

I – Integrity

> Integrity means that you take the high ground in every situation. Do not lower yourself or your standards. Commitment to personal character and principle guide you. No one should ever question whether you are a good person or not. You are what you do; so prove

133

you are a person of integrity in your conversations, behaviors and actions. You are solid and unshakable in your conviction to do the right thing. If tempted, you resist. Some believe that whatever they think or do is acceptable as long as no one finds out; they justify. This is errant thinking, as you will continue to hurt performance even if no one finds out. You know that which is wrong and that which is right. Do the right thing every time and in every situation. Even if ridiculed, you will become a better person for acting in such a manner to show others the right path. Never accept a thought or behavior that lowers your standards; always strive to achieve greater moral fortitude and strength. Others will come to rely on that strength.

M – Making a difference

Always seek to make a positive difference in your life and in the lives of others. Helping yourself and others means you avoid the obvious negatives which affect yourself and those within your influence. If you know someone who indulges too much in a negative behavior, you are enabling that behavior unless you do something positive about it. Strive to make a positive difference in the lives of every person within your sphere, especially children. They need all of your positive guidance and wisdom to face the inevitable challenges of life – elephants will confront them soon. No matter your current situation, improve your life and become a role model for a child. They look up to you and need your positive input; they need your guiding light, so shine brightly.

P – Passion for excellence

Seek excellence in everything you do. Seek a passion for life itself. There will always be something or someone that will attempt to thwart your performance efforts, if you allow it. By adopting a passion for excellence, you strive to find the way and the means to make everything better. Everything means everything; you strive to make your thoughts more positive, you strive to produce greater positive output in your health, relationships, work, and finances. You strive to become excellent in all things and all aspects of life. In your relationships, you strive to listen more and to create positive outcomes. You seek wisdom. Your desire for higher levels of quality in life is consuming. You seek to take action whenever possible to make any person, thing or circumstance better. You are proactive in taking action and solving problems to become excellent in all things.

A – Always improve

Improvement connotes measurement. To improve one must know where they have been and where they are going to take the next step in the proper direction. To improve you must "learn to learn" from your mistakes. Our missteps in life are opportunities to learn what not to do...do not continue to do the things (i.e. patterns) which yield negative results. Break the patterns of the past that have led to subpar performance and adopt patterns of success. Always improving means you know where you are in terms of each Life Category performance level at all times and seek to improve Life's Outcomes. You seek measureable improvement. Remember you are either going up or down, nothing is stagnant in life. You must press forward constantly to effectively manage change. Seek effective and timely measures of performance such that you can take appropriate action-control over your Self-System. Awareness of the consequence of every thought, conversation (internal and external), decision, behavior and action taken is critical for personal improvement. You seek to improve awareness via your measurement system and to take better control and management of Self-Leadership.

C – Compassion for others

Compassion means you are to empathize and to take positive action to comfort those who are in need. There is no lack of need for compassion. Many around you are hurting physically, mentally, emotionally, financially, etc. Those within your influence are performing at a subpar level in their Life Categories and everyone needs support energizing their Power Source.

Ask those in your sphere how they are doing in each of the Life Categories. Ask them how you can help them to be successful. When interacting with someone who may need you, use the CEO method; that is clarify the need, empathize with the need and desire to improve the current state, and offer to help. You may not be able to help, but offer anyway. Often, just the gesture of the CEO method can be enough to brighten someone's outlook. Compassion for others means you give hope. You may not be able to change someone's fortunes in a given situation, but you have the gift of hope; give it freely and genuinely.

T – Taking risks

Without risk, there is no reward, as the saying goes. You live in a world of probabilities. Without positive change, what is the probability of positive improvement? There is a zero percentage probability you will experience positive performance improvement without positive change. The Impact Performance! - Personal Improvement Model and principles presented herein constitute a guide; it is a roadmap for positive change. The intent is that you will develop a process for living that increases your probability of living a life of Impact Performance! It is up to you however. You are the person responsible for taking the next step. Are you willing to take the challenge of eating the elephant? When you overcome the challenges and obstacles in your path of success, you grow and become a stronger person. Take the risk of personal performance improvement and face that which stands in your way; eat the elephant.

"Anyone who has never made a mistake has never tried anything new."

Albert Einstein

Adoption of the Impact Mission-Values statement is a proven strategy for on-going personal improvement.

Fuel Self-Leadership

The Power to change and to sustain on-going personal improvement is a function of your ability to summon more:

- Energy
- Desire, the Will to Succeed

- Intrinsic Motivation
- Courage

You are to call upon greater amounts of energy, desire, self-motivation and courage as you eat the elephant. If it were easy, you would have likely done it already. To effect change, greater Power is required. Many of us may have goals and a well-conceived plan to achieve those goals, yet why do we fall short of our target? The answer is simple; most lack the Power to fuel Self-Leadership in which to effect change, stay focused, and break patterns to see their goals realized in the face of obstacles. Other priorities or a reversion to a previous way of living derails the best of improvement intentions. Most cower to the elephants and find a path of least resistance in which to exist; thus settling for a subpar level of performance. To initiate and maintain positive change, you need more from your Power Source.

Energy

Energy is tangible; you can feel it. You experience low energy and high energy levels and every level in-between. Some people have more energy than others do. We see others who appear tireless; they are up constantly while others appear down and lacking in energy. You obtain and expend energy every day. Increasing the baseline amount of energy a human possesses is doable. You can access more when needed.

Energy, as with time, is gone once expended. Use your energy wisely for positive gain.

Think of energy in terms of strength and agility. You will need more to conquer that which stands in your path of success.

There are three keys to gaining more energy on a daily basis: Health Performance, balance and avoiding energy drains.

Better health equals greater energy.

In terms of Health Performance and overall wellness (mind, body, and spirit), you may be thinking, "Isn't Health Performance an output and not part of the Self-System input?" This is a good observation. However, keep in mind that everything about the Self-System is interrelated and connected. When you are able to create more energy to fuel Self-Leadership, you are more capable of improvement in the Health Performance Life Category. Additionally, when you focus on and improve your Health Performance, you will experience greater energy and Power. When you improve in strength and agility in each of your physical, mental, and emotional states, your energy level increases.

Evidence is clear that when people improve their body performance, energy increases. However, it is also true that when your mental and emotional performance increases, additional energy becomes available. You have likely experienced times when you were mentally or emotionally drained, and your overall energy was consumed.

We exercise our bodies to gain greater strength and agility. It is possible to exercise our minds and our emotions as well. Improve in all sub-categories of Health Performance and more energy appears.

Balance releases energy.

Imagine you are on a tightrope. If you become unbalanced, the amount of energy expended becomes great in order not to fall. Importantly, you cannot move forward as you are attempting to regain balance. However, if you are balanced, the amount of energy expended to move forward is minimal.

We have discussed two types of balance, the balance across the Health Performance sub-categories of mind, body, and spirit as well as overall balance across the Life Categories of Health, Relationships, Career and Finances. Once you adopt a performance focus and achieve a greater level of balance, more energy releases and stressors fade. Thus, there is more energy available to make improvement progress. As you gain more control of your Self-Leadership and progress in all the Life Categories (i.e. become more balanced), more energy reserves become available.

Have you ever felt out of control in your life or unbalanced? In these times, did you expend great levels of energy to regain your balance? You may be experiencing a moment of imbalance presently; if so, regain your balance and you will release more energy to eat the elephant.

Energy dissipates quickly, if you let it.

Energy can be synergistic with others, transferred to others or taken from others. We have all seen how someone can brighten the lives or dim the lives of others.

Your well of energy drains quickly if you allow it. What is the number one short circuit? The main causal effect of energy drain is a toxic relationship. Manage your relationships with every person within your sphere of influence to avoid energy drains. It is likely that you allow people within your sphere of influence to rob you of invaluable energy. Do you allow someone in your life that is negative to zap your energy? If so, you need to push them away to a point where they can no longer have a negative impact and not consume your energy. Those who drain your energy (e.g. toxic relationships) cannot be allowed to influence you in any way, shape, form or fashion. On the other hand, seek those who energize you, pump you up, and ignite your fire of desire. Associate with those who exude positive energy. You can plug into their energy source to help fuel your Self-Leadership. Energy is transferable, plug in to positive energy sources.

Of course, there are places, behavioral patterns, and circumstances that can be energy drains as well. Physically locate yourself where positive energy flows. Spend more time in places that yield positive outcomes. Break the patterns of negative thought and negative behavior. Any time a negative thought enters your mind, eliminate it and move quickly to a positive thought such as your Impact Goals. Adjust circumstances to favor positive energy flow.

Feelings of guilt, shame, remorse, inferiority, jealously, rage, anger, revenge – every negative thought and every negative feeling will drain your energy. Make energy that is more positive available by freeing yourself of the past and make way for a brighter future. This may not be easy. Now is the time to start taking the steps necessary to eliminate the negative and accentuate the positive. Find sources of positive energy and get plugged-in.

Take a hard look at how you expend your energy. Once you eliminate the energy drains, your energy reserves will explode and you will be better prepared to manage Self-Leadership and progress in the Life Categories.

For every action, there is a reaction. As you take action, keep in mind there is a reaction; there is a resultant consequence. When you expend energy, make sure it will produce a positive result. With age comes experience and life knowledge. Expend your energy wisely, for positive gain.

A body in motion tends to stay in motion. As you move forward, it is likely your momentum will carry you forward. Be careful that the path you are on is the path towards achieving your Impact Goals. If you are on the wrong path, you will likely continue on that path and expend valuable energy until you change direction. Remember, success begets success. Get on the path of success.

The extra Power you make available via Health Performance improvement, balance and avoidance of energy drains, will fuel your Self-Leadership in order to take meaningful and positive action-control. Power fuels Self-Leadership.

Desire, the Will to Succeed

Those who possess a desire and the will to succeed are likely to demonstrate improvement. Without it, nothing happens. Even those with tremendous energy can falter without desire and without focused effort on achieving Impact Success.

Desire and the will to succeed originate from the vision of a better tomorrow for our family, others and ourselves. Recall, Elephant Eater "success" has been redefined. Success is making progress towards the Impact Goals, striving for balance across the Life Categories and adopting a performance focus. It becomes much easier to stoke the fire of desire once you establish a clear vision of personal improvement and a life of Impact Performance!

Greater levels of desire and will to succeed can be attained from seeing and emulating others who are successful. Inspiration can originate by envisioning a life where you can truly help others to succeed and fulfill your purpose. On-going motivation to succeed can come from those who are committed to your success (e.g. Accountability Partners and Mentors). No matter your age or circumstance, there are people willing to help you reach your indicated milestones along the Impact Performance! Continuum.

A means to gain more desire is to network with those whom you admire. Associate yourself with those who possess integrity. Learn more about their patterns and behaviors. From these observations, you will gain a clearer vision of where you want to take your life and how to achieve. Those who follow a positive direction and who possess the capacity to help others will inspire you.

Ultimately, desire and the will to succeed come from within. Often we refer to people with a burning desire as someone who has heart. "She has the heart of a lion." We see others achieve great things and overcome improbable odds with shear heart and the will to be victorious.

You can gain more desire and will to succeed by developing a clear picture of who you are to become. Impact Performance! is achievable. You have to want it.

Intrinsic Motivation

Motivation is broken down into two main categories, intrinsic and extrinsic. Intrinsic motivation refers to self-motivation (e.g. sense of achievement) and extrinsic motivation refers to external motivators such as money or other forms of reinforcement to achieve a desired outcome. In the context of personal performance improvement, extrinsic motivators typically do not yield sustainable improvement. The example, given earlier, is people who want to lose weight for the wrong reasons. They crash diet to lose weight only to gain the weight back and suffer mental and emotional distress as a result.

Sustained improved personal growth stems from intrinsic motivating factors. Every person wants to grow personally and achieve great things. Unfortunately, society programs us to believe that only external motivators are important and we tend to focus only on those rewards (i.e. surface-ism).

Recall the higher levels of human needs such as self-esteem and self-actualization. Each of us desires to satisfy these higher levels of human needs; it is intrinsic. In addition, we yearn for greater levels of mastery and autonomy to fulfill our purpose. Mastery and autonomy are our core intrinsic motivating factors to achieve higher levels of human need satisfaction. You can unearth the intrinsic motivators buried years ago. Daniel H. Pink's book *Drive* demonstrates clearly that intrinsic motivating factors vs. extrinsic motivating factors are the key to sustainable performance improvement. As you adopt a performance focus, improve in the Life Categories and strive for balance, you develop greater mastery and autonomy over your Self-System.

You may feel unmotivated, down or even depressed. Every person will feel down at times; this is natural. It is critical to avoid being defeated with no sense of direction or purpose. There is nothing, not a person, place, thing, or circumstance, that can defeat you. You have what it takes to be successful. So, let it out.

You can tap into greater levels of intrinsic motivation with a positive belief system, celebrating past accomplishments, and achieving improvement victories every day. When you truly believe you are a success, then your chances of ongoing success increase dramatically. It is motivating in and of itself to think you can accomplish anything. Now, look back, think of a few of your accomplishments, and celebrate. It is a rewarding feeling to accomplish anything that has a positive outcome; identify with those feelings. Make the sense of achievement and accomplishment real and tangible. These feelings are fuel for the Elephant Eater's engine. Celebrate the improvement victories you have accomplished every day; you are victorious. Every time you think something positive, use spoken words to create a positive outcome, make a positive decision, exhibit positive behavior for others to emulate and take positive actions, then celebrate and note those victories in your Impact Journal.

As you make progress, even if the progress is small but in the right direction towards your Impact Goals, it will become easier to identify with and bolster your intrinsic motivation. Develop mastery and autonomy over your Self-System and intrinsic motivation explodes!

Courage

Courage embodies many forms depending on the obstacle or threat facing you. For example, there is physical courage to face a physical threat or moral courage to stand–up for what you believe in the face of popular opposition. Courage is required to face fears, uncertainty, the unknown and threats. Every person can fuel Self-Leadership to face his or her elephants with greater courage. If it were easy, you would have already eaten the elephant, right? It takes courage to face your greatest fears.

You can summon more courage through practice. For some, it requires courage to speak in public due to their fear of making a mistake (and feeling humiliated). However, as people practice speaking in front of others, it becomes easier and easier. Videotaping those practicing to speak publicly is a helpful tool because they can see themselves in action. Another example is teaching a child to swim when they are afraid of the water. They start in the shallow end and develop a comfort level over time with deeper and deeper water as their swimming skills improve and confidence grows. Then, when their comfort level is adequate, they can swim in the deep-end by themselves with no or little residual fear. The point here is that you can take steps to conquer your fears with practice.

The two examples above are for very specific tangible activities. What do you do about intangibles such as the fear of failure, the fear of others conspiring against you, or the fear your spouse will leave you? It is a bit more difficult to practice and develop skills to overcome an intangible fear. Rather, it takes courage to have faith in something that you cannot touch, smell, or taste. Often you have to dive headfirst into the deep-end of your fears, not wade in. You have to trust and believe in yourself that you will survive (because you will of course).

Now, the Impact Team is asking to tackle your greatest fears, challenges, and obstacles that stand in your way of performance improvement. Of course, there are instances when you can practice, but in the case of breakthrough performance, you must take a risk and dive-in; simply make it happen. Do not look back. There is no fear you cannot overcome. Get moving!

Components of the Power Source to fuel Self-Leadership:

- Energy
- Desire, the Will to Succeed
- Intrinsic motivation
- Courage

You have the ability to become more aware of these components of the Power Source and to summon more overall Power from each. Sustainable improvement is a function of your ability to create more energy; ignite the fire of desire, and become more motivated and courageous. Power ignites positive change.

All components of the Power Source are interconnected. You can tap into additional reservoirs of Power to fuel Self-Leadership and eat the elephant. Once you are able to summon greater Power and take more control of Self-Leadership, you will realize that nothing can defeat you.

Exert Greater Management of Self-Leadership

Fueling Self-Leadership is a critical strategy, as you need extra Power to get moving and create meaningful and positive change. The next strategy is to exert greater management over Self-Leadership. You may be able to summon copious amounts of Power at will to create movement and overcome inertia. However, to overcome the static friction of your status (i.e. to effect positive change), you need better management of Self-Leadership.

Recall the components of Self-Leadership:

- Thought Patterns
- Decision Making Paradigm
- Behaviors
- Actions

As mentioned previously, every thought, decision, and action taken has led you to your current performance level and Life's Outcomes. You cannot change the past. However, you can effect positive change this very instant to increase the probability of positives outcomes for you and others going forward. In the context of the Self-System, when you improve the process that takes inputs and creates outputs, then you are going to improve the outputs. You can improve Life Outcomes by improving your thought patterns, decisions, behaviors, and actions.

Thought Patterns

Every great achievement by humanity started with a single thought. Likewise, every great tragedy created by humanity started with a single thought. Your thought patterns are yours, no one else's. If you have negative thoughts, then negative decisions, negative behaviors and negative actions tend to follow. If you have positive thoughts, then positive decisions, positive behaviors and positive actions tend to flow.

The mind is complex and everyone is different. We cannot address all the variations of thought, cerebral bio-chemical reactions, or responses to stimuli of the mind. Of course, there are those who are sound in mind and possess positive thought patterns while there are some who need professional help. The contention here is that you can make a conscious effort to shift negative thought patterns to positive thought patterns. Positive thoughts increase the probability of improved outcomes.

Your mind tends to follow a predictable pattern. The idea is to break any negative thought pattern, arrest the perpetrating thought, and reprogram thought patterns for positive outcomes. Further, if your mind is preoccupied with worry, feelings of despair, or regret for example, it is difficult or impossible to generate a positive thought pattern. Let negative thoughts melt away to make room for positive thoughts. Again, for those who need professional help, seek it. There is no shame in discussing your thought patterns with a trained therapist. It is their passion to help.

Practice the elimination of any preoccupying thought that is unproductive and replace it with action. Discard any thought not focused on improvement. Occupy your mind with how to make things better; become a problem solver. Has worry or despair solved a problem? The answer is no, zero. However, if you are concerned, for example, with your children's performance in grade school, then do not worry or stress; do something positive. You can become more involved in their studies, join the PTA, guide your children to see the value of learning, and instill intrinsic motivation. If you find yourself in a confrontation at work, do not allow a negative thought to enter your mind; rather, find a mutually beneficial solution; become known as a problem solver. Use your mind to solve for a better outcome in all things.

Another way to refocus is to spend some time lifting up someone else. Make a conscious effort to get outside yourself to help someone else; this act deflects the focus away from you and reinforces your capacity to help others. Acts of compassion are good medicine for the troubled soul. Acts of charity can bring you much peace of mind and joy in your heart; your negative thought patterns melt when lifting others. Helping others can quiet the most troubling of storms. Always, someone else needs your help. In good times and bad, reach out; you will feel better. Offer compassion not out of an attitude of "See what I did." Rather, help others simply because it is the right thing to do. Replace negative thoughts with positive actions.

Before you know it, you will be helping others succeed and it will come naturally. You will achieve deep intrinsic satisfaction that stimulates the Power Source. Your negative thoughts will fade and positive outcomes will result. Your decisions and actions will lead to greater results for all involved.

Do not allow negative thoughts about your health, relationships, career or finances to occur. Create positive outcomes by replacing any negative thought pattern with a pattern of positive action. When negative thoughts arise, spring into positive action.

Decision Making Paradigm

How do you make decisions today? Are you making better decisions today vs. when you were younger? Have you learned from your missteps?

No matter how old you are or your present station in life, you can always improve your decision-making paradigm. It is critical to learn from experience. That is, you should reflect on any situation, assess how you could have performed better, and apply that knowledge going forward. Then when a similar situation arises, you can improve the outcome. The ability to reflect and self-assess is an Impact Performance! improvement principle.

Most decisions are programmed by our thought patterns, as discussed in the previous section. Intuition and the influence of others often influence our decisions. We tend to acquiesce to authority in our decision-making. Whatever the case may be in how the decision you make arises, you can improve the paradigm for better outcomes.

It is naïve or vain to think every decision you make is the "right" decision. Instead, think of decision making as a life-long experiment. You know you are going to make mistakes, so plan on learning from those mistakes. Do not dwell on poor decisions and do not gloat over good decisions; learn. Every day is a learning opportunity; take advantage of your life's experiences.

In the attempt to deliver improved outcomes, the Elephant Eater attempts to make more objective and data-based decisions in all matters of importance. How you make decisions is more important than the decision itself. When one enhances their decision-making paradigm based upon better information and with the intent to learn as part on-going improvement, then the decision itself becomes secondary as the overall probability of better decisions increases.

You can make better decisions by taking more time to make a decision and with the acquisition of more data in which to make the decision. Study on a subject or consult your wise mentor before making an important decision. The better informed the decision, the greater the likelihood of a positive outcome. Additionally, if you make your best attempt, then there is no regret no matter the outcome, good or bad because you have the expectation of on-going learning.

Your decisions should be geared towards improvement in each of the Life Categories and how best to eat the elephants.

Behaviors

Behaviors reflect who we are as a person. Others see our behaviors and make judgments about us. We see our own behaviors and make judgments about whom we are. The issue is that most justify their behavior. No matter the negative effects on others and on their Life Outcomes, people tend to justify their negative behaviors.

You have exhibited patterns of behavior in each of the Life Category sub-categories. You have patterns of causal effect in your Health Performance, Relationships Performance, Career Performance and Finances Performance. The older we become, typically the more difficult it is to adjust or change these patterns of behavior. Yet, to improve performance, we must change our patterns of causal behavior.

Lack of self-awareness and caring will yield sub-optimal performance.

Self-awareness is the key to behavioral improvement. If you become more aware of your behavior's effect on personal performance and on those in your boat, then you can more accurately assess your performance. With consciousness comes clarity. Experiment with your behavioral patterns. If you change a behavioral pattern, you can clearly see the results with greater self-awareness.

Perform introspection of the patterns you exhibit in each of the Life Categories. What are your patterns of behavior with respect to your mind, body and spirit's strength, agility and balance therein? What are your patterns of relationship management at work, with family, friends and your significant other? What are your patterns of behavior in terms of seeking passion and challenge at work to become more value-added? What are your patterns of behavior when generating income, spending and investing to create more wealth and to become a role model for others? You know the patterns; write them down if it helps to map-out the behavioral pattern that leads to sub-par performance in each of the sub-categories.

You are intelligent enough to realize that certain behaviors are not productive and do not move you forward along the Impact Performance! Continuum. Yet, you continue the patterns. The reasons for continued negative patterns are your comfort level, programming and elephants. Your behavioral patterns are a way of living which yield current outcomes. If you are comfortable with your present behavioral programming and acquiesce to the elephants, then you are stuck. To move forward, you will necessarily expand your comfort zone, eat elephants and reprogram behavioral patterns.

Self-control with the ability to say "no" will yield greater Self-Leadership.

To break a pattern of behavior, you must say no to that pattern. Think, think, and think again before engaging in a non-productive behavior. If the behavior does not promote a positive outcome, then do not engage in that behavior. Break the cycle of negative behavior and negative perform- ance by telling yourself "no."

You know certain behaviors and impulses lead to negative outcomes. You need more Power to control these urges. Tap into your Power Source to avoid the behaviors that lead to negative outcomes in each of the Life Categories. You have the capacity to control behavior. Once you identify the negative behavioral patterns and begin to eliminate them, it becomes easier and easier to focus on the new behaviors that lead to positive outcomes.

When considering behavioral changes, rely on your Impact Mission-Values statement. Your behaviors reflect who you are; be a role model for others with your improved behavioral patterns. Everyone will appreciate the positive outcomes and begin to emulate your positive behaviors; be a leader.

Actions

Thoughts lead to decisions and the subsequent actions taken. We are responsible for our thoughts, decisions and actions. No one takes the test for us; no other person controls our emotions, our conversations or goes to work for us. We own the actions that lead to our present performance levels. Actions are an outward expression of our decisions; we think something, we decide what to do, then we act. We own our actions.

For every action there is a reaction; there is a consequence. The more capacity to foresee consequences of actions taken, the more capable you are in controlling actions for positive gain. Think about certain situations where you said or did something which led to a positive outcome. Try to replicate it. It is important to evaluate your conversations and actions each day. As appropriate, capture those conversations and actions and the resultant outcomes in your journal. How could you have performed better today? What could you have said or what could you have done today such that tomorrow will indeed be a better day for yourself and those in your boat?

How do you manage your actions for improved outcomes? In carpentry, there is an old saying, "Measure twice, and cut once." As you go forward, measure the consequences of your spoken words and of your actions at least twice before speaking or acting. Have you ever spoken or interacted with a truly wise person? They do not say superfluous words or convey meaningless ideas. They tend to teach us with important points about how to move forward; they are problem solvers. The wise are deliberate in their actions; they are not impulsive, as they understand that actions have consequences. As you attempt to manage Self-Leadership, seek the wise and become wiser in your thoughts, decisions, spoken words and actions.

Rely on your Impact Vision and a performance focus when considering each action you take. Each spoken word and action should be to create a positive outcome and lead you towards the indicated milestones on the Impact Performance! Continuum of each Life Category.

Measure Performance and Take Action-Control

"It is of no profit to have learned well, if you neglect to do well."

Publilius Syrus

A primary premise of Impact Performance! is measurable and demonstrable personal performance improvement. When Elephant Eaters speak of eating the elephant, we refer to demonstrated elimination of elephants and the resulting improvement along the Impact Performance! Continuum. Measurement is the key strategy for performance improvement; otherwise, how will a person know "improvement"?

We have suggested three principle components of your Impact Performance! measurement mechanism: Journaling, the Accountability Partner's feedback, and advice from Mentors. The implementation of these measures affords a means to indicate tangible improvement.

Measurement is meaningless without action-control. If you measure performance, yet do not take corrective action, what is the point, correct? Action-control is the on-going process to take immediate steps to improve your Self-System upon measurement of its performance. If you measure the depth and responsiveness of your Power Source (input) and dimension a gap in Power Source performance, take action to improve your ability to summon more Power at will. If your Self-Leadership (the process) is not functioning properly upon inspection, take corrective action. If your measurement system is not delivering accurate and timely information, take action to improve its function.

The process of measurement and action-control affords on-going improvement of the Self-System. Improve each component of the Self-System. Improve your Power Source (input), Self-Leadership (process), and the measurement mechanism on a continuous basis to yield greater Life Category performance (output).

The purpose of measurement is to indicate appropriate action for improvement.

At this point, we have presented general strategies to eat the elephant and to achieve measurable personal performance improvement. The strategies presented overcome the friction of your current state and provide momentum. In the following section, we will discuss specific tactics you can employ to achieve on-going performance improvement.

Employ Elephant Eater tactics

Here we present tactics that Elephant Eaters employ to start eating the elephant and realize tangible improvement results. Some of these tactics may appear to be obvious, and some are indeed obvious. However, it is necessary to list them here as a reminder. Suggestions for improvement are given below per each Life Category sub-category. Subsequent to the sub-category tactics, overall performance improvement tactics are presented.

Elephant Eater Impact Performance! Tactics

Health Performance Tactics

Impact Goal: To become healthier, to achieve greater strength, agility and balance in mind, body, spirit

Physical

Control physical stress to grow in strength and agility. Treat your body as a temple. You possess only one body.

1. Determine your percent body fat, and work to achieve a healthy percent body fat for your age and height. Increase the amount of protein and reduce the amount of saturated fat in your diet. Diet is the easiest and most controllable factor that leads to improved physical performance. 75% of physical performance is related to diet. Consult your primary care physician or nutritionist as appropriate.
2. Join a Wellness program.
3. If you suffer from a chronic illness, join a disease management program. Most health insurance plans offer disease management as part of your health benefit package.
4. Exercise daily. This includes cardio to increase the heart rate.
   a. Stretch all major muscle groups daily; as we age, flexibility becomes more important than muscle mass.
   b. Go for a walk, a hike, a jog (for at least 20 minutes of elevated heart rate) every day.
   c. Lift free weights when possible, but do not overdo it.
5. Consume a low fat, high protein diet.

  a. Consume more protein.
      i. One 8 ounce glass of milk = 8 grams of protein
      ii. Three ounces of chicken breast = 24 grams of protein
      iii. Three ounces of fish = 24 grams of protein
      iv. One protein shake = up to 40 grams of protein
  b. Avoid fried food; seek high fiber foods such as fruits, vegetables, and whole grains.
  c. Avoid processed meats (e.g. hamburger).
  d. Supplement with vitamins (a daily multi-vitamin is suggested). Speak with your doctor or nutritionist about dietary supplements.
6. Sleep – new research suggests sleep is more important than once believed.
7. Do not consume tobacco.
8. Do not consume alcohol (or at least only less than five ounces in a week).
9. Monitor and track percent body fat. Use a commercially available percent body fat scale (less than $50).
10. If in great shape, compete. Participate in charity events (e.g. a 10K run to support heart disease research).

Mental

Conduct controlled stressing of the mind. Stimulate the analytical and the creative – grow in strength and agility.

1. Take a break from what you do during the day and focus on an analytical exercise for 10 – 15 minutes (e.g. play Sudoku or a game of chess).

2. Take a break from what you do during the day and focus on a creative exercise for 10 – 15 minutes (e.g. read a fiction novel, daydream, write, paint, etc.).
3. Meditate – free your mind of thought; take 15-20 minutes of quiet time (silence) daily.

Emotional

Conduct controlled stress of the spirit – grow in strength and agility.

1. Take an Emotional Intelligence test online; understand your ability to identify, assess, and control your emotions.
2. Find minimal stressful people, places or circumstances and do not react; do not react to that which stimulated a negative emotion in the past; simply do not react. Listen to your inner speech, but do not react. Later reflect on the emotion and your ability to control that emotion.
3. Practice (2) above with greater levels of stressful people, places and circumstances once you demonstrate the containment of negative outward emotional responses. Practice, practice, practice the ability to control your emotions.
4. Identify the emotional state of others via active listening and asking how someone feels in a given situation. Be careful not to inflame a situation by asking someone how they feel if you know already it is a tense and heightened emotional state.
5. Never overreact to any situation; stay calm – there is a difference between an emotional outburst and a passionate debate.

6. Share your emotions with your Accountability Partner and Mentor. Discuss how best to control your emotions given the most emotional of stimuli.
7. Read articles and books on how to control emotions. Seek professional help as needed.

Relationship Performance Tactics

Impact Goal: To manage my relationships for mutually beneficial outcomes, to better manage who is in my boat

Work

1. Seek written expectations of performance from those who consume your energy and time.
2. Review performance weekly or monthly (agree on specific performance metrics), chart your weekly or monthly performance and gain agreement from your supervisors on corrective actions.
3. Ask if you are meeting expectations in every meaningful relationship. Seek to find mutually beneficial outcomes. Ask and give feedback regarding progress in all meaningful work relationships.
4. Ask how you can be more productive and effective in your communications (verbal and written).
5. Categorize those people with whom you find to be difficult; do not allow them to affect you. You have priorities that are more important in your life (i.e. your Impact Goals).
6. Ask your boss and co-workers how you can help them to become more successful; then help them.

7. Avoid those who are politically motivated that can torpedo your efforts to become more value-added.
8. Identify who is in your "work-boat" and bring them closer to you.

Family

1. Exude compassion for your family members. Ask them how you can assist them with their distressing situations. Then help them.
2. Discuss their performance and ask how you can help them succeed; identify your role.
3. Ask for their help in pursuing your Impact Success; for those committed to your success, invite them into your boat.
4. For those who pose an energy drain, push them out of the boat to a distance far enough from you to avoid negative influence.
5. Identify who is in your "family-boat."

Friends

1. Assess whether those closest to you are helping you to become successful; share your Impact Mission-Values statement and your Impact Goals; if they are committed to your success, invite them into your boat; if not, then keep them at arm's length.
2. Review the advice your friends offer; write it down. What has been the outcome? If positive, then accept their advice; if negative, reject their future advice. Seek advice from those who are truly wise.
3. Clearly establish expectations in every friend relationship.

4. Identify who is in your "friend-boat." Bring those friends who lead to positive outcomes closer to you.
5. Ask your friends how you can help them succeed. Lead your friends to greater levels of personal performance via your behaviors and actions.

Significant Other

1. Practice Couplism.
2. Communicate, communicate, and communicate each other's expectations and any frustrations that may exist. Be willing to bend your behaviors and actions to meet your partner's expectations if possible.
3. Be nice. Do not fight. Discuss to create a mutually beneficial outcome.
4. If not in a committed relationship, open your heart to the possibility. The right person will come into your light when you shine brightly.
   a. Do the activities you enjoy.
   b. Associate with people of integrity; expand your network.
   c. Adopt a performance focus.
   d. Help others and spend time on charitable activities; this is a great way to meet like-minded people.

Career Performance Tactics

Impact Goal: To find passion and grow in my profession, to become more value-added

Challenge

1. Work as hard and diligently as possible to create more value for your company and yourself.
2. Seek mastery in your work; seek additional training, and train yourself on new technologies, products and services in your organization.
3. When appropriate, ask for more responsibility.
4. Understand the competition. How can you help your company be more competitive?
5. Join a professional society.

Passion

1. Find exciting aspects of your work. Write down the aspects of your work for which you have passion.
2. Create new work opportunities which excite you. Join a committee or form a committee regarding something for which you have passion.
3. Start a family day, a green day, or perhaps reduce the carbon footprint at your work.
4. Pursue the hobbies that bring excitement. Involve your spouse. Is it possible to create revenue from your hobbies?
5. Create new opportunities to help others at work become more successful (e.g. teach a class on new sales techniques or new computer applications).
6. Teach others about personal performance improvement.

Finances Performance Tactics

Impact Goal: To become a responsible steward of my finances and build wealth, to become a role model for others

Net Worth = Assets - Liabilities

Income

1. Generate multiple streams of income (e.g. seek an additional job or sell your hobbies online).
2. Seek advancement to higher levels of responsibility at work, which offers more income.
3. Start an online business.

Spending

1. Create a budget and stick to it.
2. Say "no" to impulse spending; think twice before making any purchase.
3. Use coupons; check online for discounts.
4. Buy generics (e.g. mouthwash, medicines).
5. View your household as a company; do not spend a dime unless there is a clear return on the investment.
6. Do not spend money to impress anyone (e.g. expensive dating habits or a new car).
7. Pay-off your credit cards; stop using them. If you cannot pay cash, then go without.
8. Strive to keep your debt to income ratio as low as possible (below 30% is a good target, which includes the mortgage).
9. Teach your children the value of frugal spending habits.

Investing

1. As above, cease the use of credit cards; pay cash for purchases.
2. Pay-off your credit cards. The interest rates are very high. It is like an investment to eliminate them. Consolidate your debt into one card at a lower interest rate if possible and focus on paying it off as quickly as possible.
3. Pay-off any other remaining or outstanding debts.
4. Repay anyone who has ever lent you money.
5. Open a savings account (typically credit unions offer better savings rates).
6. Refinance the mortgage to achieve a lower interest rate (seek a 20 year or less term on the loan).
7. Fully fund your company's 401K to maximize their contribution.
8. Fully fund your IRA.
9. Do not purchase a new vehicle unless the interest rate is zero or exceptionally low; assess the resale value and the operating costs of any vehicle purchase (i.e. maintenance and gas mileage).
10. Carefully evaluate insurance policies and long-term care policies to determine which route is best for you and your family.
11. Give to charity. Giving is a tenet of Impact Performance!
12. If you have the ability to create a job, do it. The gift of dignity through work is honorable.
13. Read books on money management; begin to teach your children about the time-value of money and the principles of money management.

The above action-oriented tactics are suggestions meant to help you focus on concrete steps you can take to demonstrate improvement in the Life Categories. Many other tactics may be helpful in delivering early improvement progress. Do whatever it takes to move forward. You are on a quest to demonstrate personal performance improvement. You can take a suggestion from each Life Category and work it today. **Get moving!**

Overall Elephant Eater Tactics

- Believe in yourself – no one else will believe in you if you do not at least try to believe you can improve your performance.
- Practice positive self-talk – focus your inner conversations on achievement and problem solving. Say it out loud, "I will improve my performance in Health, Relationships, Career, and Finances." Then, say it repeatedly until you actually believe it. Your spoken words convey beliefs, thoughts and meaning.
- Practice visualization; see yourself as a winner; imagine positive outcomes in every conservation and action you take.
- Avoid vanity; it is not about your appearance or looking good in a given situation. It is about demonstrated performance improvement and helping others.
- Seek to help someone daily.
- Change your perspective:
  o Do charity work (e.g. donate some of your time to a homeless shelter).
  o Go to an orphanage and hold an orphaned baby.
  o Devote time at an assisted living facility.
- Never waste time with worry or despair; become action oriented.

- Turn the television off; spend more time with family (outside if possible).
- Avoid the obvious patterns and actions that lead to negative outcomes.
- Never procrastinate; you have a checklist, get busy.
- Laugh, have some fun, enjoy the journey of performance improvement.
- Take a day of rest and relaxation.
- Celebrate your victories. You have earned it.

Your Attitude as a Performance Improvement Tactic

Go from negative to positive. If depressed, seek help. What is the surest way to defeat negative thoughts? Adopt a performance focus. Block negative thoughts with thoughts directed towards your Impact Goals and specifically on eating the elephant. If a negative thought presents itself, spring into action towards achieving your milestones. Go for a jog; do anything to create activity. It is Ok and natural to get down on occasion but never become defeated. Bend but do not break. Remember you can achieve great things in your life; you can demonstrate progress, be a "success," and help others to achieve improvement. If you have followed the steps outlined in Bites #1 through #6, you are successful. Keep going; you can do it.

You have the gift of conscious thought and the ability to improve your life and the lives of others. Do not waste the gifts of life bestowed upon you. If you need an attitude adjustment, then think about those who are afflicted with debilitating diseases such as Alzheimer's, Parkinson's, or Lou Gehrig's (ALS). Those people and their families have no choice but to manage the best they can. If you have the choice, then choose a positive attitude and a positive belief system. Remember, anything is possible.

We have stated it before, but it is so important we will state again. If you believe you cannot achieve, you are likely to fail because you have accepted defeat before even making the attempt. If you believe you can achieve, your probability of significant performance improvement increases dramatically. Your attitude and belief system regarding personal performance facilitates a free means towards achieving your Impact Goals. A positive attitude, the ability to learn from your missteps, and performance focused effort will yield performance improvement. Your positive attitude is a performance improvement tactic. Be positive, work hard and positive outcomes will materialize.

Recall your improvement strategies of Bite #7: The Eat the Elephant Impact Action Plan:

- Live the Impact Mission-Values Statement Daily,
- Fuel Self-Leadership,
- Exert Greater Management over Self-Leadership,
- Measure Performance and Take Action-Control,
- Employ Elephant Eater tactics, and
- Strive for Balance.

Thus far, we have discussed all strategies except for Strive for Balance. This final strategy is pivotal for on-going improvement. Note we did not suggest achieving balance. It is difficult to achieve absolute balance as life is ever changing with people and events knocking us off course constantly. Thus, we suggest striving for balance daily across the Life Categories. This means to be cognizant of the need for balance and make every attempt to progress along the Impact Performance! Continuum for each Life Category daily.

Strive for Balance

We have discussed balance earlier. Here we are simply reinforcing and stressing the importance of balance as a strategy for overall improvement.

It is important to remember balance as you engage the Power Source and focus your Self-Leadership on the Impact Objectives and milestones. If you focus solely on one sub-category and do not address the others, then your progress will be slow and you may become frustrated. You need to put effort into making progress across the four Life Categories, as there is synergy in your efforts. The Life Categories are interwoven. You will gain greater momentum with focused strategies and tactics across all of the four #1 elephants of the Life Categories, which stand in your path.

It is easy to defocus if you are not balanced. Energy will dissipate; you cannot move forward and your ability to face the Elephants diminishes. Conversely, balance affords forward momentum and greater Power; stressors fade.

When you make progress in one Life Category, you can more easily improve in the other categories, as they are interconnected. The forward movement in Health Performance will help you progress forward in all other Life Categories. The same is true for all Life Categories.

When you strive for greater balance, the stresses tugging at you will lessen. With less stress, your forward momentum increases. If you perceive an imbalance or a threat to your balance, then act quickly to mitigate that threat. Balance is paramount to Impact Success.

Given the strategies outlined in the Impact Action Plan, you have concrete objectives, milestones, strategies, and tactics to guide you. Balance across your improvement efforts affords a piece of mind. As you make entries in your Impact Performance! Journal and note the progress in each Life Category, your level of personal satisfaction and sense of achievement will explode on the pages.

Recall that Impact Success is demonstrating improvement in each of the Life Categories, a performance focus and striving for balance. Balance your improvement efforts across the Life Categories and the probability of breakthrough achievement is greatly increased.

You have completed the seven bites of the Impact Performance! – Personal Improvement Model (IP!-PIM).

Congratulations! Now it is time to get moving and live a life of Impact Performance! Nothing, not even an elephant can stand in your way. You have the Power, the tools, the plan and the support team to conquer anything. You have the utensils to eat any elephant standing in your way; dinner is served.

Here is the great news: once you effect positive change and begin to see progress, you will look back and smile with a deep sense of personal satisfaction, contentment, and a hunger for more.

Volo Essum Barrus! (Latin translation for *I want to eat an elephant!*)

Next, the Scott and Elaine story exemplifies Couplism. You will likely relate to aspects of this Impact Performance! story.

5

Couplism

Elaine and Scott's Dining Experience

On a Friday night in the spring, it was Elaine and Scott's first date night in over three months.

Scott yelled out, "Are you ready yet? The baby sitter is here and the clock is ticking!" Elaine was thinking to herself, "Isn't this supposed to be a romantic evening? I want to look beautiful for Scott; after two children, it isn't easy." Elaine responds, "I'll be down in a few minutes."

Elaine walked down the stairs in a new blue dress with a low neckline showing off the pearls Scott had given her on their ten-year anniversary last year. Elaine had gotten her hair trimmed and highlighted, and her nails manicured earlier in the day; she wanted this night to be special. She knew that her marriage was far from perfect and was deteriorating. Scott had been preoccupied with work and obviously stressed-out lately. She had never seen him like this before. He was different. She questioned whether she had changed. Was she different? Were they growing apart? Over the years, she had seen several of her friends' marriages fall apart and the devastating effects on those families; she did not want her family destroyed. She thought, "What can I do? Am I not attractive anymore or desirable? Am I not the wife Scott wants me to be?" She and Scott had not been intimate for months.

Scott saw Elaine as she entered the foyer and his heart leapt; she never looked so beautiful, as he gazed upon her. His raw desires peaked. Scott had not felt this way in years, he thought to himself. At the same moment, his heart sunk as his feelings of inadequacy surfaced and overtook him. His job was stagnating, the credit card debt was mounting, and he had not spent quality time with the kids in forever, it seemed. Both children, Josh and Megan, were in sports and he had not been to a game in almost a year. He was not sure how long he could last in the current situation; he felt trapped. He had seen some of his friends who had cheated on their wives and bragged about being with someone younger, more attractive and how it made them feel. Was he missing out?

"Ok Scott, I'm ready," she said. "Let's go" was the solemn reply. There was not much said as he drove their late model Acura TL to their favorite upscale restaurant along the waterfront. Elaine was excited because he had not told her where they were going. She recognized the restaurant where they were headed when he pulled off the exit. This was to be a great night, she thought.

As they were seated, Elaine could tell something was bothering Scott. She asked, "What's wrong honey?" He wanted to talk about his troubles but felt that if they talked about it, another fight would ensue. They had been quarreling much too frequently in the past year and snide remarks were becoming the norm. They had not had a pleasant conversation in so long that both were unsure of what it was like; they had lost the ability to have fun together. "I'm okay, what is wrong with you?" was his retort.

Her night was collapsing before it truly began. She knew it was probably hopeless, but she wanted it to be romantic, just like it was when they were dating - a time full of hope and joy. How could they return to a loving relationship? She wondered, how?

He ordered their all-time favorite bottle of wine (priced at $129). She recalled the weekend in Napa they had spent after one of Scott's business conferences in San Francisco. Elaine had become accustomed to the finer things in life that Scott had always tried to provide. She worked part-time in a legal firm as a paralegal. This provided some extra income and gave her more free time with the children. Elaine was attractive and had a bubbly personality. She drew much attention from the male co-workers, which tended to offend the female co-workers. She liked the attention especially from the younger single male lawyers. She had not received much affection from Scott lately, so any male attention made her feel wanted. Scott was a sales manager for a firm that provided accounting software. His mid-sized company had done well in the past but had lacked the foresight to stay in the lead with the fast-paced change and innovation in the industry. He was well respected, but sales were trending downward and some of his long-term clients were leaving. His job was on the line. She said, "Oh that is my favorite. Remember our weekend in Napa?" She smiled glowingly. Exasperated, he thought, "How can I afford this night? The baby sitter plus the dinner will cost me an arm and a leg...and she'll probably want to go somewhere after dinner too!" Even though Scott knew they could not afford to spend the money, he wanted to please

Elaine. "Yes that was one of our best weekends together." She believed this might be a great night after all.

Scott and Elaine had met at a fundraiser, a Run for the Cure 10K event that supported cancer research. Elaine was an event coordinator; she was in her first year of college. Her mother had died of breast cancer that previous year. This was her way of remembering and honoring her mother. Scott was athletic, a track star in high school; he believed the 10K was an opportunity to see if he "still had it." They met just after the race. Scott had pulled a hamstring muscle and needed assistance. Elaine was there for him.

Their dinner was filled with small talk about the kids and their schooling and sporting events. They talked about the state of the house (which was in need of several repairs) and they talked about their aging parents. Elaine had mentioned that her best friend had just purchased a new SUV. The friend described in glowing detail how she enjoyed the comfort and ride of a new vehicle. Scott's feelings of inadequacy grew with each topic of the conversation. "I got my hair done today. Does it look nice?" she asked. In her mind, he should have commented on her new hairstyle, as she had not felt this pretty in a very long time. "Oh yes, you look beautiful, gorgeous actually." She was reassured. Scott felt even more insecure.

"Dessert?" the waiter asked. Scott gestured to Elaine for her response, being polite to afford her the first response. "Yes, I'd like the raspberry tort, please." He said, "None for me, thanks, I'll just take a bite of hers." He thought he could at least save a few dollars by denying a dessert. When the waiter brought the check, Scott gulped; he knew that they had spent too much. The bill with tip was going to be over $250; he grimaced. Elaine had little idea of the financial woes they were experiencing as Scott had always paid the bills. She knew they always paid the mortgage on time, the children lacked for nothing, she drove a nice car and that Scott had a 401K at work. There was no issue, right? She had never been concerned with money or spending; she grew-up in an upper middle-class family but never learned about finances or money management. Scott came from a hard-working blue-collar family of modest means. In his early career, he did exceptionally well as a regional salesperson and joined his current firm five years earlier as a sales manager with great promise and expectation. Their spending outpaced the reality when they bought the bigger house and the new cars. As his income tapered-off, their spending habits continued. Now they were in trouble, but in denial.

"That was wonderful. Thank you." she smiled lovingly. "Yes dinner was great; that wine is the best." he replied. "Can we walk along the waterfront?" she asked. "Great idea," he said, and thought.

Elaine was feeling better about the night, but she could tell that Scott was not happy; he was not the charismatic top-of-the-world Scott she fell in love with…. What happened? She wondered as they walked along the water. "Scott, I know that something is bothering you and things are just not the same between us. We do not talk anymore, as we used to. You work all the time and go play golf on your free time. We do not seem to be together as a family anymore. You used to kiss me like it was our last kiss; I miss that." Elaine wanted to open up an honest discussion, but Scott took this question as a slap in the face.

"You just don't appreciate how hard I work and the things you get; you are never satisfied! Most women would kill or die to be in your shoes!" How could she be so bitchy after all that he had done for her? "I just spent $250 dollars on you and you want to start a fight, is that it? I cannot believe you! If you want a kiss, then where are you? We sleep in the same bed; kiss me!"

Elaine replied heatedly, "You haven't made love to me in months. Is there someone-else? What's going on Scott?"

"I can't believe you are going to ruin this night and accuse me of cheating. What is wrong with you?" He shouted.

"Take me home," she said with tears welling in her eyes; she felt defeated. Scott realized the situation had gotten the best of him. Worse, he did not know how to communicate with the woman he loved, his wife. He felt defeated.

On the drive home, Elaine's emotions ran high, and then low. She thought that Scott just was not there for her emotionally anymore. It seemed they were no longer partners. Could she depend on him to be there? She felt as though her life equated to money, nothing more. She had never heard Scott refer to money before. Were they having money problems? She wondered, but was afraid to ask. She felt even more defeated as he did not confide in her.

The next day, there were no spoken words. Scott had slept in the guest room the night before to avoid any more arguments. He did not want to argue with Elaine, but he did not know how to tell her how he was really feeling. He knew he had overreacted the night before.

Both went about their business as if they did not know each other. That afternoon, Elaine took the kids to a birthday party in the neighborhood. She did not invite Scott to go. He went to his home office and tried to figure out how he could pay all the bills and maintain their standard of living. He was depressed. He knew he could not rely on any miracles at work. Something had to give. He called his father, Ted, for advice.

"Son, you've got to get control of your family life; sounds like you're in a tough spot."

"I know Dad, but how do I get out of this mess? I don't want my family to fall apart. I just don't know what to do. I blew up at Elaine last night and we both knew at that moment we could not go on like this. Dad I could see it in her eyes. She is unhappy."

"There is a guy at work, Mike, who mentioned a good technique for helping people to improve their lives. He is into that kind of stuff. Maybe it will help. Give him a call, okay?"

"Ok dad, I'll give him a call."

"Let's get together Saturday and talk about it once you've had a chance to find out about this..." Scott's dad said with authority.

"Sure thing, I'll drop by next Saturday around noon."

Elaine confided in one of her neighborhood friends, Shirley, at the birthday party about the fight she and Scott had the night before. Shirley told her that she thought Scott was cheating and that she might want to get out before the kids got older. Elaine remembered Shirley saying, "All men cheat; life is too short to be miserable girlfriend." Shirley had been married and divorced twice before, drank heavily and referred to men by how she met them and what they did for her.

"I've been on three 'sport dates' in the last two weeks!" Shirley said proudly while laughing aloud and spilling her drink. "The airport guy took me on a dinner cruise, the desperate guy from accounting bought me flowers and he took me to the new French restaurant downtown, and, oh yeah, the good-looking 20-something broke gym guy took me to the music festival last weekend. They all call and text me, but if I don't want to see them, I just let them keep trying. It is great to be in control!" She said as she continued to laugh while sipping on her cocktail. Elaine was full of doubt more than ever and wondered what to do.

Elaine and Scott barely spoke that evening and into the night; both had contemplative moods. "Good night," Elaine said, hoping Scott would open up or apologize about the night before. "Good night," Scott said, and went to sleep without saying another word.

Scott headed-off to work the next morning. He had a busy day with an on-going restructuring of the sales staff. The salespeople were not going to like it, but upper management demanded this change, and Scott was to implement this new strategy. He knew several of his best salespeople would leave due to the changes. He was as stressed-out as he had ever been in his life. The non-speaking situation with Elaine was hard on him and it only made things worse overall. He relied on Elaine as a friend. What happened to them?

Elaine was distraught as she dropped the kids off at school. She did not work on Mondays. She wished that her mother were still alive to give her some real motherly advice. Instead, she called Scott's mom, Celia, with whom she loved dearly and trusted. Celia always considered and treated Elaine as if she were her own daughter but never tried to interfere with Elaine and Scott's marriage or the parenting of the kids. Celia always offered support and good advice in the past. "Hi Mom, this is Elaine. Can you have lunch today?"

"Yes, I've got a few things to do this morning, and then we can meet. Are you okay?" asked Celia. They had gone to lunch on Monday's often, but Celia could tell by how Elaine asked the question, that something was wrong.

"Yes, I'm okay. I just need your advice. Can we meet at Chauncey's about 11:45?" asked Elaine. "Of course sweetheart, I'll see you then."

Elaine said earnestly to Celia, "I have never seen Scott so stressed-out. We've been quarreling over nothing lately, and I'm worried we may have financial problems. We fought Friday night and haven't spoken since."

Celia replied with concern, "Every relationship has its ups and downs. You and Scott must talk about this."

"We don't talk at all anymore." Elaine felt like crying.

"Don't give up Elaine, Scott is a good man. Both of you will have to focus on the things that are truly important to both of you and renew your love for each other every day. Ted and I learned years ago that we have to work together and strengthen each other to become one, not two people living under the same roof. If you are having financial problems, then you have to be part of the solution. Don't let Scott think he's alone on this; get involved."

"Thanks Mom, I just don't know how. It seems we've grown apart." Elaine had never felt this way before; she was as vulnerable as she had ever been.

"Find out what is truly bothering Scott and work together to solve it. Your lives together are not separate; they are one. You'll need some courage but you can do it, I know you can, I love you, and don't want to see you hurting like this." Celia knew that Elaine would have to take a step that she had never taken before, a step towards saving her marriage.

"Mom, I'll do whatever it takes."

"Ok sweetheart, start with forgiveness."

"What do you mean?" asked Elaine while wiping a tear.

"You forgive yourself and renew yourself. You forgive Scott and you ask for his forgiveness. Renewed love begins with forgiveness." Elaine's heart was full. She knew there was hope.

"Thanks Mom, thanks for being there for me."

"Of course Elaine, I am always here for you and for Scott."

Celia offered, "Let's get together Saturday." Celia knew that Ted had spoken with Scott the day before.

"Sure! Let's get together this weekend and talk again. I can bring the kids over Saturday, if you want."

"Hello Mike, this is Scott. I'm Ted's son." Scott called Ted from the car, rushing from the office to get some lunch.

"Well hello Scott, Ted said you might give me a call."

"My father said you are into self-improvement and may be able to give me some advice."

Mike replied, "If I can help, I will. What seems to be the issue?"

"Everything, it seems, I am stressed-out at work, the finances are slipping, and most importantly, my family life is suffering."

"When is the last time you got some exercise?" asked Mike.

Scott replied, "Well I used to be in great shape, a runner actually, but I haven't even jogged a mile in a couple of years."

"It seems you're a bit out of balance Scott."

"That's an understatement!" Scott replied jokingly.

"Look Scott, most people experience imbalance and a loss of focus at some point in their lives. You are not alone or unique in this situation. The great news is that you can turn things around fairly quickly, if you truly want it."

"Well I am getting pretty desperate at this point; I'll try anything, even counseling, whatever it takes."

Mike replied in a fatherly manner, "If you want to improve, then you will, but you'll need some help and a determined focus; counseling may be part of the solution, we'll see. I want to help."

"Thanks Mike, where do I start?" Scott said anxiously.

"Come by the office on your way home. I'll give you a book which will help. Let's start there, okay?"

"Will do, Mike. See you around 6:00 pm."

Scott arrived home around 6:45 pm; he had been working late recently, so this was no surprise to Elaine. She had already picked-up the children from school and had dinner with them. They had played on the trampoline with friends across the street at a neighbor's house. Now they were settling down to complete their homework assignments. Elaine, remembering Celia's advice, embraced Scott as she had when they were first married. He was a bit shocked, and dropped the book he got from Mike and gave her a bear hug. They did not speak. They moved back from each other and gave a reassuring look to each other. "Scott, I want to talk, okay?" asked Elaine.

"Yes, I want to talk, too. I want to spend some time with the kids tonight, and then we'll talk when they go to bed."

Elaine bent over to pick up the book that Scott dropped and asked, "What is this?"

Scott replied, "I got this book from Dad's friend at his work. He said it helps to provide a performance focus and balance in people's lives." Scott hesitantly added, "I thought maybe it can help us?"

Elaine said with a spark, "That's great sweetheart; let's talk about it tonight." Scott was reassured.

The children were asleep by 9:30 pm. As they got into bed, Elaine said, "Scott I want you to know I love you. I have always loved you and dreamt of our lives together, our home and growing old together. However, right now, we are not being good to the kids or ourselves; we have to turn things around. For us to move forward, we have to forgive each other and ourselves for everything we have done or said that has caused grief or pain. It may take some time but I want our love to be renewed. I want us to begin loving each other as I know we can. I know it can be great again."

"I agree," Scott replied in a resigned tone. "I love you Elaine. Our home...our family...this is my life. There is nothing more important to me. I am sorry I snapped at you after dinner the other night. Let's work it out, okay?"

Elaine felt a sense of relief and comfort knowing that they were going to try to work it out. "What do we do now?"

"Well, this guy at Dad's work, Mike, said that couples should read and practice this book together. He called it 'Couplism'. I am not sure what that means but I thought we should try it. It's called *Eating Elephants*. Mike said that elephants are what hold you back. Mike is some kind of a self-improvement nut. Dad likes him, so I thought, why not, right? He said that if you follow these principles, adopt a performance focus and strive for balance, you'd be more successful. I am skeptical but thought if we tried this together maybe things will get better for us."

Elaine replied, "It's worth a shot. Let's read it together."

Scott pulled into the driveway. He was taken aback by the site of Elaine's car in the driveway. What was she doing here? He thought she was taking the kids to the park for the afternoon. Had his Dad set this up? Scott got out of the car and walked to the back yard where his dad, Ted, was chipping golf balls. Josh and Megan were playing in the back yard and ran to hug him before running off again. Scott looked in the kitchen window and saw his mom having coffee with Elaine. "Dad what is Elaine doing here?"

"She's having coffee with your mom."

"Ok, but what is she doing here? I thought we were going to talk?"

"Yes, son, we're *all* going to talk." Ted said with a strong tone.

As Scott walked into the kitchen from the back porch, Elaine's eyes widened. "Everything okay, honey? I thought you would be playing golf today."

"And I thought you were taking the kids to the park...I came over to talk with Dad."

"I came over to talk with Celia."

Both chuckled. Scott announced, "Ok, now you've got us here, what's this about?" Ted and Scott took their seats.

Ted leaned over and kissed Celia on the cheek. "Scott, Elaine, we know you're having trouble. Now, we're not going to interfere. We just want to help." Ted explained.

"Dad you've already helped us. Elaine and I have started reading that book Mike gave us. It is not really a book. It's more like a guidebook on how to live a life of Impact Performance! It has actually helped us to realize we need to focus on what is truly important and to achieve balance in our lives. We're not finished; we just started reading it this week, but we're reading it every night when the kids go to sleep," Scott explained proudly.

"Mom, we took your advice and committed to forgiveness and renewed love for each other. We are not looking back. We agreed that before we say or do anything, we are going to think, 'How is this going to help us and our family?'" Elaine said confidently.

Celia and Ted were beaming; they were not sure how the conversation would go that afternoon, but were prepared for the worst. "Both Celia and I know you're going to try your best."

Scott replied, "Dad it's not just about trying your best. It's about results. Elaine and I, we are a couple. We are one, a team. As time goes by, you will see why we are so enthusiastic. We are going to eat the elephant and demonstrate improvement in our lives; we are going to live with Impact Performance! together."

Ted had not seen this level of commitment or confidence in Scott since his track days in high school. Trying to contain his excitement, Ted offers, "If you need anything, we are here for you."

Elaine replied, "Don't worry about us; we're going to be just great. We need and appreciate your love and support very much."

Ted leaned over to Scott, "What's an elephant? Tell me more about this book, son."

Within a couple of months, Elaine and Scott's Impact Performance! Couplism efforts came alive. They now:

- Declare to experience Couplism and live a life of Impact Performance!
- Live the Impact Mission-Values statement.
- Post their Impact Goals, Impact Objectives (the "eat the elephant dates") and milestones on their refrigerator. They journal every day.
- Agree to strive for balance in their lives and demonstrate improvement across all Life's Categories.
- *Improve Health Performance* and gain greater strength and agility; Scott runs again and Elaine takes a Pilates class. They agree there would be no more emotional outbursts; they are a team.

- *Improve Relationships Performance*. They allow only those who are truly committed to their family's success into their boat. Elaine does not listen to Shirley any longer and Scott does not pay attention to the guys in the office who try to justify their negative behaviors. They communicate expectations and express their love daily.

- *Improve Career Performance*. Scott finds greater challenge and passion in his career with a new marketing position that allows him to spend more time with his family and utilizes his talents more effectively. Elaine has decided to go Law School, which was her dream. She had given up that dream to marry Scott.

- *Improve their Finances Performance*. Elaine came to realize her impulsive spending habits were causing great financial strain on the family finances. With the money she saves from simple purchasing habit changes, she is able to start tax-free college funds for the kids. Her focus changed dramatically. Scott sold his new SUV for a used vehicle for more cash flow.

Additionally, they:

- Agree on using visualization to envision their future and adopt a performance focus full of positive self-talk.
- Realize they were their biggest elephants and now think and act less selfishly.
- Identify the people, places, things and circumstances standing in their way; they identify their elephants together. They commit to eating their elephants together and holding each other accountable.

- Avoid the obvious improvement pitfalls and now see positive results with their positive attitudes and new perspectives.
- Realize Scott's linear thinking forms patterns that lead to negative thoughts. As such, he now uses positive self-talk and meditation to eliminate negative thoughts all together.
- Cut discretionary spending in half. Yes, they still have date night, but now they are both responsible for the finances and spend only that which is budgeted. Scott no longer feels the need to impress Elaine with an expensive dinner. She is content with his emotional commitment. Elaine realizes there are more important aspects to life than being entertained. Her contentment is the progress she sees in the growth of her family and its togetherness.
- Energize their Power Source and exert more control over their respective Self-Leadership.
- Became each other's Accountability Partner; they became best friends again based upon mutual respect.
- Scheduled uninterrupted time for each other and for the kids.

Scott and Elaine realized they were successful and now celebrate their on-going improvement success. They are making demonstrable improvement; they can see the charted results on the Impact Performance! Continuum and in their journals. They strive for balance across the Life Categories. They are now performance focused with greater Power Source and Self-Leadership. Mike became Scott's mentor and Celia for Elaine. Both Scott and Elaine make journal entries together every night. They now live a life of Impact Performance! together and celebrate Couplism.

On a Friday night in the fall, it was Elaine and Scott's date night.

During dinner at a modest chain restaurant (iced tea and no dessert), Elaine looked lovingly into Scott's eyes. "We're making it Scott. I love you so much. It's better than I ever imagined." They had spent the day together as a family, watching Josh and Megan's soccer games in the morning and then going on a hike in the park that afternoon before dropping the kids off with Scott's parents. Elaine felt even more love for her husband when she saw his devotion to their kids.

Scott replied, "I know we are. It's where we need to be honey. I love you with all my heart."

"Remember, the kids are staying at your Mom and Dad's tonight..."

6

Get Moving!

"To give anything less than your best is to sacrifice the gift."

Steve Prefontaine

Why not begin living a life of Impact Performance! today, at this very moment? Are there any reasons not too?

There are no excuses. None. Remember you are responsible for your success. Instead of lamenting about your situation, do something about it. You have identified the elephants that hold you back and you have sage advice on how to proceed in eating the elephants and to improve in each of the Life Categories. Importantly you have the capacity to help others to succeed as well. You know what you need to do. You need to Get Moving!

Our existence is finite; our time limited. We are mortal and do not know when the end shall come. As such, treat each moment as a precious gift. Our time is fleeting. Why waste a moment of your precious gift on any thought or action that is not for positive gain in your life or in the lives of others?

As each day passes, that day of your life represents a greater portion of your remaining lifespan. Tomorrow is a greater percentage of your remaining time on this earth than today. What are you doing today to ensure that the impact you make tomorrow is greater than the impact you deliver today? Importantly, what greater gift is there than to make a lasting positive change in the lives of others, such that your legacy of Impact Performance! will live on?

There is zero rationale not to make a positive difference in your life starting this very moment. Institute a process for positive change today. Get moving!

7

The Dessert,
The Sweet Taste of Success

Success begets success. Confidence begets confidence. Once you begin to experience performance improvement momentum, keep going to achieve true breakthroughs in personal performance. Over time, you will gain more and more self-awareness of your Self-System, and how to manage on-going Impact Performance! Importantly, you will develop mastery across the Self-System. With experience, you will master your Power Source and Self-Leadership to yield greater Life Outcomes in the Life Categories. You will master the use of your measurement system to actuate action-control for on-going performance improvement.

With mastery comes purpose; pursuing your purpose yields mastery.

As you meet your Impact Objectives and move forward along the Impact Performance! Continuum, you will realize you are meeting all of Maslow's Hierarchy of Needs. Mastery over your Self-System yields greater satisfaction of all your basic needs including self-actualization.

Pursuing Impact Performance! is a self-fulfilling positive experience. There is no downside to pursuing a life of Impact Performance! As you eat the elephant and practice the Impact Performance! principles, the old way of living and its subpar performance outcomes become clear. You will see progress and those in your boat will enjoy your success as well.

Success is striving to reach your Impact Goals, striving for balance and a performance focus. It is not more difficult or complex than that. The great news is that anyone can be a success by this definition. All anyone must do is to try. This book provides you the guidance, model, and motivation to put you on the path of Impact Success. Always celebrate the sweet taste of success. You have earned it.

8

Never Dine Alone, Join the Hunt

"No man is an island..."

John Donne

Recall one of the major reasons most do not maintain the gains of personal performance improvement efforts is a lack of support. Impact Performance! offers online support to Elephant Eaters through our blog: http://blog.ip-getmoving.com and Facebook page:

www.facebook.com/impactperformance

You may be inspired by this writing and make an earnest attempt to improve your Power Source, Self-Leadership and to eat the elephants for improved Life Outcomes. However, without a strong support system, on-going motivation may be lacking. We recognize this scenario and offer online support. It is critical to your ongoing success to engage those in your boat, your Accountability Partner and Mentor for much needed ongoing motivation. They are to remind you that positive outcomes stem from positive change.

Not to be too philosophical here...every person is connected; we are connected by our desires, our strengths and our weaknesses; we are human. We cannot live a life of Impact Performance! by ourselves. Surround yourself with like-minded Elephant Eaters to support each other. If you are in a committed relationship, we encourage you to practice Couplism. There is no better way to gain motivation than to give it.

So, learn and practice the principles outlined in this book such that you may join the hunt to help others eat the elephant.

9

From Elephant Eater to Elephant Hunter

"No one stands taller than when they bend over to lift others."

Joel Osteen

Believe in someone before they become successful. Everyone needs inspiration to achieve. You have the gift of inspiring others to achieve what they once believed impossible. As you demonstrate mastery over your Self-System, you gain the recognition and badge of Elephant Eater, for you ate the elephant. Your belief in another person and the ability to help them achieve Impact Success is a higher purpose in life.

An Elephant Eater who has mastered his or her life can become an Elephant Hunter. The Impact Team is comprised of Elephant Hunters who assist Elephant Eaters. If you are interested in delivering a greater level of Impact Performance! to others, you can become a recognized Elephant Hunter by the Impact Team. Please contact us for details. The best way to sustain mastery of the Impact principles is to reach-out and teach others.

Of course, the ultimate measure of your life's success is to help others to succeed. The reward of helping others is not measured in the number of thanks, pats on the back, or some expectation of monetary gain. No. Your reward is to fulfill your purpose as a human being. Humanity is truly about helping your fellow man, woman, child, the sick, the hungry, the poor, the elderly, and the indigent.

Our hope is that you will achieve mastery of your Self-System, achieve Impact Success and live a life full of Impact Performance! Importantly, we hope that you will help others and fulfill your purpose. Please share your Impact Performance! success stories with us at:

www.ip-getmoving.com

The greatest deed is to help others succeed.

Epilogue, Author's Note

Is this the point of your life, at this very moment, where you thought you would be or the person you imagined? No matter the point you find yourself today, you can make an Impact. We have presented a model that delivers Impact Performance! No matter what you do with your life, we urge you to improve all aspects of your life, adopt a performance focus and strive for balance. That is, to be successful and live a life of Impact Performance!

The major premise of this writing is that you can improve your life by eating the elephants that stand in your way and hold you back. The biggest elephant is you. You must change in a positive direction to yield positive outcomes. It is up to you to summon the Power needed to better manage Self-Leadership and demonstrate improvement in each of the Life Categories.

Another key premise of this writing is measurement. Performance cannot be improved without an accurate and timely measurement mechanism. Seeking feedback from yourself (journaling) and others (Accountability Partner and Mentors) will allow you to see progress and take appropriate improvement actions. Sustained improvement requires on-going support and motivation that you can find among those in your boat. Remember to allow only those who are truly wise and committed to your Impact Success to influence your Self-System.

We all desire to become relevant and achieve significance. As you make progress in the Life Categories of Health, Relationships, Career and Finances, you will experience more Self-System control and your purpose will reveal itself. We offer the Impact Performance! - Personal Improvement Model as a means to point you in the right direction. Ultimately, we hope you will grow and master your Self-System to the point where you can help others achieve Impact Performance!

When facing a challenge or fear, break the issue into smaller components, which are more manageable. Then tackle the smaller components of the issue and make progress. Use your source of Power to fuel Self-Leadership (positive thoughts and actions) to yield positive outcomes in your Health, Relationships, Career, and Finances. Ongoing Impact Success is your ability to develop a process for ongoing improvement and ability to eat any elephant that appears.

Our desire is to help a broad audience attain meaningful and sustainable personal performance improvement. There is great challenge in modifying a person's current way of thinking, patterns of behavior, and actions to yield improved personal performance. However, we have seen impressive and dramatic personal performance improvements using the IP!-PIM and the Impact principles outlined herein.

We have witnessed ordinary people accomplish extra-ordinary feats in their lives and in the lives of others. We have seen these ordinary moths turn into exceptional butterflies.

Exceptional people:

- Do not make obvious errors in judgment, behaviors, actions
- Learn from their mistakes
- Do not make excuses

- Solve problems
- Control their emotions
- Possess perpetual optimism and perpetual positive self-talk
- Possess the ability to constantly improve Self-Leadership and their Power Source; they measure performance and take action-control
- Are balanced and maintain a performance focus
- Have the will and the courage to face any challenge or fear
- Eat elephants for breakfast, lunch, dinner
- Hunt elephants so that others can succeed
- Live a life of Impact Performance!

Exceptional people are not born exceptional; they are created from lessons learned, hard work, and perpetual optimism. You possess everything it takes to become truly exceptional; make it so!

Time will not forgive that which is wasted. Get moving!

Appendix

Toxic Relationships

Additional Quotes

Suggested Reading

Personal Declaration

My Life Category Goals

Toxic Relationships

It is a naive romantic notion to believe that every person with whom we interact is "normal" and treats us, as we deserve to be treated. Remember the Golden Rule, "Treat others like you want to be treated." It is broken all the time. The point here is to identify toxic behavior and eliminate toxicity from your improvement efforts. Toxic people are Elephants; they are in your way of achieving Impact Performance!

Are there people in your life who leave you drained emotionally, mentally and perhaps financially? You may be the most positive person, but when you are interacting with that person, you feel the positive energy evaporating.

Here we will discuss a variety of characteristics of toxic people. In each, these cases of psychological disorder seek enablers; those who feed into the other person's neuroses. Some people are so desperate for social interaction and social acceptance that they tolerate toxic relationships. It seems perverse, but when exposed to the toxicity for long durations, the "sane" person becomes addicted to the toxin (enabler's syndrome). When removed, they seek to replace that toxin with another similar toxin; another toxic relationship, and the cycle continues as they become toxic. As with drug addicts, when the addicting drug is removed, the addict seeks to replace it. Have you ever witnessed a sane person become "crazy" (e.g. delusional) due to the influence of someone's toxic nature?

It is dangerous to your overall wellness to tolerate toxic relationships. Importantly, you may recognize enabler's syndrome as an elephant. You cannot achieve significant personal performance improvement given such a negative influence as a toxic relationship. They are toxic to your happiness, your mental state and to your self-esteem. They suck the life force out of you and even shorten your lifespan. Toxicity attacks the Self-System. The only known anti-dote is removal.

If you recognize any of these toxic people, then tactfully move them out to a point where they cannot influence your Self-System. Do not allow the people described below to influence your Power Source or Self-Leadership in a negative way as negative Life Outcomes will result.

<u>Toxic personalities:</u>

It's ALL About Me: An extreme sense of self-importance and belief that the world revolves around them (i.e. vanity). They are overt about getting what they want and pout when they do not get it (e.g. childish behavior). You want to say to them, "It isn't always about you."

Toxicity: They are solely focused on their needs, leaving your needs unmet, as they do not care about your needs. It is a one-way street. You are left disappointed and unfulfilled. Further, they zap your energy by getting you to focus so much on them, that you have nothing left for yourself.

Me, Me, Me: Similar to the above. You can never give enough to these people to make them happy or satisfy them. They take you for granted and have unrealistic expectations of you. They find ways to continually fault you and never take responsibility for anything themselves.

Toxicity: You spend so much time, effort, and resources (i.e. money) trying to please them that you end up losing yourself in the process (and your shirt). They require all of your time and energy, leaving you worn out and your own needs sacrificed. They are parasitic and will find another host when you are gone. You are to say, "Good riddance!"

Mr. / Ms. Manipulative: These people are proficient at manipulation tactics. You may not realize you have been manipulated until it is too late. These individuals figure out what your 'buttons' are, and push them to get what they want.

Toxicity: These people eat away at your belief system and self-esteem. They find ways to make you do things that you do not necessarily want to do. You lose your sense of identity, your personal priorities and your ability to see the reality of the situation. The world becomes centered on their needs and their priorities.

The Bummer: These people cannot see or appreciate anything positive in life. If you tell them that it is a beautiful day, they will tell you about the impending dreary forecast.

Toxicity: They take the joy out of everything. Your positive outlook on life becomes clouded with negativity. Their negativity consumes you. If not weary, you start looking at things with gray colored glasses yourself. They drain your energy.

The Judge: If you perceive something as positive, they see it as negative. If you like someone's style, for instance, the "Judge" will find it distasteful.

Toxicity: Judgmental people are much like The Bummer above. It is always a struggle interacting with them; you feel as though you are always "defending" your position.

Spending a lot of time with these types can inadvertently convert you into a judgmental person as well.

The Dream Killer: Every time you have a bright idea, these people tell you why you cannot do it. As you achieve, they try to pull you down. As you dream, they are the first to tell you it is impossible.

Toxicity: These people cannot see what could be; rather, they only see what is. Further, these individuals eat away at your self-esteem and the belief in yourself. Positive change occurs from trying new things, innovating, dreaming, and thinking out of the box. Avoid these people like the plague.

Insincere: They cannot be sincere. You say something humorous; they give you a polite laugh. You tell them you are excited about something and you get a very ho-hum response. They are blinded by surface-ism.

Toxicity: Those who are not sincere or genuine build relationships based upon superficial criteria. This breeds shallow, meaningless relationships. When you are really in need of a friend, they will not be there. When you need support, they would rather see you fail or make a fool of yourself for a laugh.

The Back-stabber: These people say or do things at the most inappropriate times and in the most inappropriate ways to make you look bad. This person is a friend who you confided in and uses your secret against you. This may be a family member who puts their nose into your affairs when it is none of their business. Perhaps, a colleague says demeaning things about you to make them look "good."

Toxicity: These people have no sense of boundaries and do not respect your feelings or your privacy. These people will cause you to feel frustrated and disrespected. They gossip about you and stab you in the back.

All of these personalities have several things in common:

1) The more these people get away with their behavior, the more they will continue. They seek enablers. They cannot see the negative result of their behavior; the enablers reinforce it.

2) Unfortunately, most of these people do not see that what they do is wrong and as a result, talking to them about it is meaningless; you feel as if you are the crazy one. In fact, they desire for you to be perceived as the crazy one to justify their behavior - bizarre, but true.

3) Most of these people's toxic behavior worsens with age. The negative impact on others intensifies over time, if you allow it to happen.

Life is too short to spend your time contending with toxic behaviors in others. Avoid spending time with people who are indicative of these behaviors described above and you will gain more Power. If you have enabler syndrome, you will need to break that pattern, of course. This may require some professional help.

Note if you see yourself on the toxic personality list above, then reread *Eating Elephants, Living a Life of Impact Performance!* Then read it again.

Toxic people are not allowed in your boat. Learn to identify these toxic behaviors and avoid the toxicity. You will be much happier. Surround yourself with positive and truly wise people. Invite only those who are committed to your Impact Success in your boat.

Additional Quotes

"We can't solve problems by using the same kind of thinking we used when we created them."

Albert Einstein

"How you think about a problem is more important than the problem itself – so always think positively."

Norman Vincent Peale

"I am not bound to win, but I am bound to be true. I am not bound to succeed, but I am bound to live by the light that I have. I must stand with anybody that stands right, and stand with him while he is right, and part with him when he goes wrong."

Abraham Lincoln

"I do not think much of a man who is not wiser today than he was yesterday."

Abraham Lincoln

"I'm going to work so that it's a pure guts race at the end, and if it is, I am the only one who can win it."

Steve Prefontaine

"One man gives freely, yet gains even more; another withholds unduly, but comes to poverty. A generous man will prosper; he who refreshes others will himself be refreshed."

Proverbs 11:24, 25

"From its exploration, the solution is only part of the reward; we gain strength and agility in learning."

Lee Alan Hord, Sr.

Suggested Reading

Maximum Achievement by Brain Tracy

Financial Peace by Dave Ramsey

Change your thoughts - Change your life by Wayne Dyer

The Seven Habits of Highly Effective People by Steven Covey

When Will My Life Not Suck? by Ramon Presson

The Five Love Languages by Dr. Gary Chapman

The Solomon Secret by Bruce Fleet

Personal Declaration

I will not be defeated. I will redefine success and I will be successful. I will live with a performance focus and balance my life. I will demonstrate positive outcomes and help others succeed. I will not sacrifice the gift of life. I will live a life of Impact Performance!

My Life Category Goals

Health

> *To become healthier, to achieve greater strength, agility and balance in mind, body, spirit*

Relationships

> *To manage relationships for mutually beneficial outcomes, to better manage who is in my boat*

Career

> *To find passion and grow in my profession, to become more value-added*

Finances

> *To become a responsible steward of my finances and build wealth, to become a role model for others*